WORLD OF GENE KRUPA

That Legendary Drummin' Man

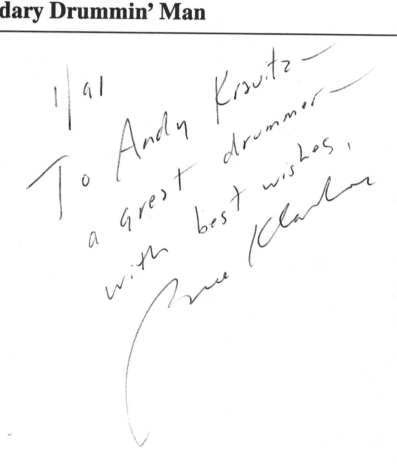

1/91

To Andy Krivitz —
a Great drummer —
with best wishes,
Bruce Klauber

WORLD OF GENE KRUPA:

That Legendary Drummin' Man

BY

BRUCE H. KLAUBER

WITH AN INTRODUCTION

By

MEL TORMÉ

Pathfinder Publishing
of California
458 Dorothy Ave.
Ventura, CA 93003

WORLD OF GENE KRUPA:
That Legendary Drummin' Man

By

Bruce H. Klauber

Edited By: Eugene D. Wheeler

Published By:
Pathfinder Publishing
of California
458 Dorothy Avenue
Ventura, CA 93003, U.S.A.

Library of Congress Cataloging-in-Publication Data
Klauber, Bruce H., 1952-
    World of Gene Krupa
    Includes bibliographical references.
    1. Krupa, Gene, 1909-1973. 2. Drummers
(Musicians)—United States—Biography. I. Title.
ML419.K78K6 1990 786.9'165'092 [B]   90-7158
ISBN 0-934793-28-X (Soft)

DEDICATION

For my musical heroes: Gene Krupa, Buddy Rich, Charlie Ventura, Milt Buckner and Bernard Peiffer; and in memory of Charles M. Klauber.

GRATEFUL ACKNOWLEDGEMENTS

This book could not have been written without the cooperation of the following: Mel Tormé, George T. Simon, Charlie Ventura, Teddy Wilson, Eddie Wasserman, John Bunch, Marty Napoleon, Carmen Leggio, **down beat Magazine** president Jack Maher, former **Metronome Magazine** publisher Robert Asen, **Modern Drummer Magazine** editor/publisher Ronald Spagnardi and art director David Creamer, **International Musician** editor J. Martin Emerson, **Variety** editor Syd Silverman, CBS Records, The Putnam Publishing Group, **Esquire Magazine,** The Slingerland Drum Company, the Avedis Zildjian Company, Charles Stewart, Duncan P. Schiedt, Michael Montfort, Steve Brockway, Academy of Motion Picture Arts and Sciences, Los Angeles Musician's Union A.F. of M. Local #47, New York Musician's Union A.F. of M. Local #802, The Microform Department of the Philadelphia Public Library, Susan Ball, and to the other authors of much material herein: Leonard Feather, Rudi Blesh, Barry Ulanov, Burt Korall, Dom Cerulli, Bernie Brown, Jack Lind, Willis Conover, John Tynan, and Nat Hentoff.

All **down beat Magazine** excerpts and articles reprinted with special permission of **down beat Magazine.**

All **Metronome Magazine** excerpts and articles reprinted with special permission of Robert Asen, for **Metronome Magazine.** All **International Musician** ex-

TABLE OF CONTENTS

FOREWORD

BY MEL TORMÉ

FOREWORD

BY MEL TORMÉ

In 1940 I was 15 years old and growing up on the South Side of Chicago. Three blocks away from where I lived was a street called Kingston. One block up from Kingston there existed a corner grocery store, replete with green awning. I used to walk over to that store a few times a week, just to stare at the awning. On it, in faded white lettering, were two names: LYKKE and KRUPA. Gene's family owned that store and the sheer magic of those five letters — K-R-U-P-A — acted upon me like a magnet.

Like every other aspiring young drummer in the country, the very mention of the name "Gene Krupa" conjured up images of excitement, glamor, jazz and that conglomerate of white pearl Slingerlands and burnished Zildjian cymbals that set this neophyte percussionist's heart soaring.

I had met Gene as a child, when I was appearing in kid vaudeville units in and around Chicago. He never spoke down to me, never treated me with anything other than kindness and encouragement. I started playing drums in the Shakespeare Grammar School Drum and Bugle Corps when I was eight. By the time 1937 rolled around and Krupa had made history with Benny Goodman, I was as obsessed with being a drummer as anyone in America.

There is an old gag in our business: "Hey, man! Didja hear? Cootie left the Duke!" (Inevitably to evolve into "Chubby left Woody, etc.") When Gene left Benny to form his own band in 1938, it was no joke. Speculation was hot around our school. Would Gene make it as a bandleader? Who would he get to play in his band? And what about

Benny? What? Davey Tough? Replacing Krupa? Oh yeah, he keeps great time but...replacing KRUPA?

'Krupa cost me a bike, the only one I ever had. My aunt Ruth bought me a Roamer bicycle for my 13th birthday. My family, like every other Depression era family, felt the terrible squeeze of the fractured economy, and a bike like that was a genuine luxury. My best pal, Vic Grenock and I took the Roamer on a shakedown cruise the Saturday following my birthday. Destination: the Tivoli Theater on Cottage Grove Avenue to see a new Bob Hope movie, *Some Like it Hot*. Debuting in that film was the brand new Gene Krupa Orchestra. I chained my beloved new bike to a lamp post right in front of the Tivoli. Vic and I sat through two shows, tapping our feet and pounding the seats in front of us in time to *Wire Brush Stomp* and *Some Like It Hot* and *The Lady's In Love With You* and *Jungle Madness*. When we walked out of the darkened theater into the fading light, the Roamer was gone. Never another bike, but I saw that movie again and again. It turns up on TV occasionally, re-titled *Rhythm Romance* for obvious reasons.

When I moved out to California with my folks, toward the end of WWII, the Hollywood Palladium was in full swing. Gene's band played there regularly and every night I saw them there, and that was **every** night, Gene let me sit in with the band on drums. A red letter day (actually night) in my life was that evening when he asked me to join the band as alternate drummer. By then I had a vocal group called the Mel Tones and was unable to accept his offer. Wish I could have.

During the war, he had forsaken his now-famous heraldic bass drum monogram with the familiar "GK" painted in large, black relief, and opted for a patriotical-ly-devised rendering in red, white and blue, with bombers in the center of the head, encircled with the motto: "Let's Go America—Keep 'Em Flying." His drums took one hell of a beating not only from his virile drumnastics but from the constant travelling, setting up, breaking down of the set, the throwing of tom-toms and snare drum and bass drum in and out of fiber cases. Yet he seemed to retain the same set of drums for years at a time. When I asked him why he didn't order a new set from Slingerland, he smiled and said: "Are you kidding? These drums are just broken in." "These drums" were six years old. When I became a

Slingerland user and endorser, "Bud" Slingerland and eventually Don Osborne, Sr. told me that they had to practically beg Gene to accept new drum sets. He never took unfair advantage of the fact that he had virtually "made" the Slingerland Drum Company and that his name, over and above anyone else's, was SYNONYMOUS with the word "drums."

Gene Krupa was as much a gentleman as he was a musician. The men who worked for him happily attest to this. Unquestionably, he was eclectic. He gleaned from the likes of Zutty Singleton, Chick Webb and perhaps even Baby Dodds. The thing is, he developed a style of playing that was comprehensible and copyable. That's what most of the drummers of the day, particularly the white drummers, did. Buddy Schutz aped Gene. So did the early Louis Bellson. Even young Buddy Rich incorporated several of Gene's "licks" in his outings with the Artie Shaw band in 1939. Like Ray McKinley, Jo Jones and Ray Bauduc, he was a highly musical drummer, not perhaps so much during his tenure with Benny, but afterward, with his own band.

In 1970, during a TV special in which we both participated, he told me how much he loved the music of Frederick Delius, an English composer who wrote, during the late 19th and early 20th Century, some of the most beautiful orchestral music imaginable. Since Delius is, coincidentally, my favorite composer, Gene and I talked animatedly about him for over an hour. Krupa was superknowledgable on the subject. He really was an appreciator, a connoisseur and authority on music of all sorts, not merely a dabbler.

One night, in 1982, Benny Goodman came in to see me while I was appearing at a New York night club called Marty's. Between shows, I did something I have always wanted to do; I sat and talked with BG for over an hour about the old days. I was surprised to learn that he did not particularly care for the convoluted, avant-garde arrangements during the "forties" period of his band; that he did like Mel Powell's playing, composing and arranging was no great revelation. Fletcher Henderson was his all-time favorite arranger for the Goodman band, and that thirties band was closest to his heart.

Drummers?

"How about Davey Tough, Benny? Harry Yeager, Buddy Schutz? Sid Catlett? Buddy Rich? Louis Bellson? They all played for you at one time or another. Who was the best?"

Benny smiled patiently. "Gene. Gene was the best. There was no one like Gene."

Amen.

HOW THIS BOOK WAS WRITTEN

This is not intended to be a biography or an oral history in the conventional sense. As I approached this subject I realized that a straight biography could not do justice to Gene Krupa. Too many biographies are dependent upon simple conjecture and opinion, with the rest devoted to resolving conflicting facts, family backgrounds and the analysis of attendant data. And little of it has to do with music!

Gene Krupa was a star and an innovator and was universally loved as a human being, but of more significance in this case, he was a thoughtful, intelligent, studied and articulate man who could easily write or verbalize his thoughts on his music, his drumming, musical study, dealing with an enforced slowdown and adapting to it, the trumped-up drug bust, etc. Even in the various interviews Gene did, the answers read like a true oral history without the posturing and exaggerations found in the words of some swing and pre-swing era personalities. He remained diplomatic, to be sure, but there was not a question he wouldn't seemingly answer and there is no reason to believe everything he said was not 100 percent truthful.

It is for these reasons that in the biographical section of this work, Gene Krupa tells his own story, done via a method of chronologically compiling and later editing Gene's interviews for **Metronome, down beat Magazine,** books, other periodicals and radio and television interviews. Gene Krupa's words were not changed. The only "editing" done was in effectively combining comments from all of the above sources, which sometimes entailed switching, in mid-sentence, from a 1950 interview to a 1972 interview in order to amplify a point or find a more descriptive reference. Because this method was used, a "Primary Source" listing can be found at the end of each biographical section, rather than footnoting each sentence (or in some cases, word), which would have been somewhat unreadable. Gene Krupa's words throughout this work are in italics.

Of course, Gene Krupa doesn't answer all the questions we might have wanted to ask him, so this project is fleshed out with some "personal conjecture," comments from Gene's musical sidekicks over the years, reviews of his working bands from 1938-1970, interviews with six of Gene's more important musical associates, a collective personnel listing, selected discography and filmography. Several pieces Gene wrote himself for **Metronome** and **Esquire** are reprinted verbatim because of their importance, as is the **Metronome** "Blindfold Test" of 1950, the Krupa-Rich session for Voice of American Radio of 1956, the **Metronome** articles which covered the Krupa-Goodman breakup and reconciliation in 1938, Krupa's comments to George T. Simon in the notes to the Columbia record, *Drummin' Man*; and lengthy Krupa interviews regarding the big-band business slowdown.

I would like to think that Gene Krupa would have agreed with my approach. But, as self-effacing and truly modest as he was, he would have probably suggested that his music speak for him. I hope that this project, taken in tandem with the large body of music he's left, finally does tell the whole story.

THE LEGEND OF GENE KRUPA

No, Eugene Bertram Krupa probably wasn't the best or fastest drummer who ever lived, but as Buddy Rich once told me in a moment of candor, "There is no such thing as the 'greatest' or 'fastest' in music. It's impossible. There might be some kid standing on the corner in Iowa who nobody ever heard of who's better than everyone."

But indeed, in any of the arts, especially music, fastest or best or loudest or trickiest or subtlest do not constitute the stuff of legend. With all that in mind, let it be said at the outset that Gene Krupa, both during and after his time, remains one of the certifiable and recognizable legends of music, jazz and otherwise.

Defining any intangible, like trying to answer the question "What makes a legend?" is nearly impossible. In Krupa's case, he was a showman, yes, and certainly a personality—why else would Hollywood cast him as an actor, drummer and bandleader in more than a dozen films?—but it was not the showmanship of the musician or leader who also sings, dances, tells jokes, and wears funny hats. Krupa made a visual impact, what with his gum-chewing, frenetic movements, knocked-out expressions and grimaces, sweating and grunting, with hair flying and sticks twirling all the while under the light strobe. But that was the extent of what the critics called "showmanship." Let us remember that musically, with one or two brief and minor exceptions, Krupa never compromised the music in which he believed. And whether one was enamored of the Krupa style or not, what he believed in was American jazz, in all its forms. At the very least, through his years with Benny Goodman's band, leader of two swing bands from 1938 until 1951, single attraction with jazz at the Philharmonic and Trio and Quartet leader until his death in 1973, the musical integrity of Gene Krupa remained wholly intact.

Let us concede that it was, perhaps, through the striking visual impact that Krupa affected the general public — even those who never liked jazz before or since — but light shows or "showmanship" notwithstanding, we must consider Gene Krupa, the innovator. He was the first to insist upon using the then-unwieldy bass drum as a part of the drum set in the recording studio in 1927. He made the drums a solo instrument, and in the process, elevated the percussionist to a position of respect, one to be regarded as a musician, not a ninth-class citizen. There were further innovations. Krupa was among the first bandleaders to prominently feature the arrangers and instrumentalists of the then revolutionary sound of be-bop in his big band. No, Krupa himself didn't make the percussive transition with total success, but he introduced to America the bop arrangements of Gerry Mulligan, Eddie Finckel, Budd Johnson and Neal Hefti and instrumentalists like Mulligan, Buddy DeFranco, Lenny Hambro, Urbie Green, Frank Rosolino, Dodo Marmorosa, Charlie Ventura, Red Rodney, Don Fagerquist and singers Dave Lambert, Buddy Stewart and Anita O'Day.

He was a pioneer in other ways. He insisted that trumpeter Roy Eldridge play in the band's trumpet section beginning in 1942, with Eldridge thus becoming the first black player to perform regularly as a part of a white band, not just as an "added attraction" or featured soloist as were Lionel Hampton and Teddy Wilson with Benny Goodman's organization. Krupa always gave public credit to the drumming innovators responsible for him, like Baby Dodds, Zutty Singleton, Dave Tough and Chick Webb, thereby educating his own admirers in the process and casting the limelight away from himself. He could have taken all the credit, but didn't. He respected, encouraged and always talked about other drummers. His insistence on thorough musical study was constant. He had time for everyone. Mel Tormé, perhaps, said it best when he described Gene as "an angel."

And there were tragedies. A divorce in 1941, a messy drug case and arrest in 1943 which would have destroyed lesser men's careers, the death of his first wife, Ethel; the struggle to keep up the big band; dealing with the strain of music's modernization in the fifties, a heart attack and subsequent variable health after 1960, breakup of a second marriage, his forced slowdown, etc. But he continued to play, and he played well through it all while still living up to the title of "legend." And "angel."

Gene Krupa is a legend not, perhaps, for the validity of his music, his innovations or because he was a nice guy. The figure of Gene Krupa, forever hunched over the marine pearl Slingerland drums and grimacing in the spotlight, was charismatic, larger than life, and yes, magic.

I saw him and met him in later years when poor health had slowed him down, and other drummers could probably accomplish with one hand what Krupa did with two. But he still had that magic and he still had that charisma. He had it when he made his final public appearance with Benny Goodman in August of 1973, two months before his death. And this has nothing to do with innovations, music, study, or fastest or best. This intangible, this magic — from wherever it might come — this is what makes a legend.

Had Gene Krupa not existed, I doubt whether contemporary American music would be played the way it is today. Sure, others might have come along and certainly, others did. And maybe they were faster, more modern or more subtle. But they were not Gene Krupa. They were not legends.

THE
STYLE OF
GENE KRUPA

CHAPTER ONE

THE STYLE OF KRUPA

The work of the late Gene Krupa should be obligatory study for today's serious drum student and, indeed, may offer some refresher lessons for a few old pros.

Rupert Kettle.

If I beat out my wildest drum solo and the people couldn't dance to it, I'd really be shocked; for I learned years ago that you just can't break time.

Gene Krupa.

Krupa's evolution as a timekeeper and soloist can be broken down into four distinct periods: 1) as a sideman in Benny Goodman's band and as leader of his own First Band until 1943; 2) as leader of his more bop- influenced band until 1951; 3) as small group leader in the early fifties; 4) as small group leader from the mid-fifties until his death.

Within the Goodman ranks and as leader on his own until 1943, there was nothing particularly revolutionary about Gene Krupa as a timekeeper. In terms of influence as a timekeeper, Jo Jones' use of the hi-hat cymbals in the early Count Basie band was about the most "revolutionary" aspect of any drumming during that time. Basically, Krupa kept his time behind soloists and ensembles using both sticks on the snare drum: as Krupa himself has described elsewhere in this work, playing "1-2-3-4" with the right stick on the snare drum and accenting on "2 and 4" with the left stick. Certainly, there were other snare drum intricacies interspersed throughout, rim-shots, other accents on the tom-toms or small crash cymbal and a bit of hi-hat work. Nevertheless, it was the relentless, rather heavy and certainly four-square use of the bass drum in the Goodman band and small groups which helped fire-up and drive those ensembles. But whatever was done was done with flash and verve, and even before Krupa took his first solo of any extended nature, the Krupa flash and verve almost commanded the spotlight.

Krupa's innovation came about via bringing the drummer to the forefront, via his recording of *Sing, Sing,*

Sing with Goodman. It was his tom-tomming interludes on that original recording which basically represented the first "extended" drum solo of any kind ever recorded commercially. Krupa's work on *Sing, Sing, Sing* had certainly been directly influenced by his study of the African Dennis-Roosevelt Expedition records, which featured the drum rhythms of Zulu natives in the Belgian Congo. And the late jazz historian, Dr. Marshall Stearns, even wrote that the Krupa tom-tomming was African in origin. However, it is generally acknowledged that African drumming has little to do with the rhythm or feel of jazz. It was Krupa who modified the rhythms he heard and gave them a jazz "feel," though one can't help but presume Krupa listened at length to the drumming of the colorful Sonny Greer within Duke Ellington's "jungle bands" of the late twenties and early thirties. But consolidation of styles or not, by way of his soloing and the personality he brought to it, Krupa brought the drums out front and proved they could be as much of a solo instrument as any other.

After striking out on his own as leader of his own band until 1943, the Krupa style of timekeeping did not evolve to a great extent, though more hi-hat work began to creep in on some ensemble passages, and there was more of an element of sensitivity in terms of dynamics. But naturally, since the leader was a drummer, Krupa was more in the limelight as a soloist — though he never hogged that spotlight — which included liberal amounts of the tom-tomming of the *Sing, Sing, Sing* variety on numbers like *Blue Rhythm Fantasy*, as well as much more use of the snare drum and rim-shot accents on it, which can be traced back to Krupa's probable main influence, Chick Webb. The Krupa solo style, which he began to perfect in those days, was mostly based on dotted quarter notes — rhythmically, almost the same as Coleman Hawkins' improvisations on tenor saxophone — with ringing rim-shots thrown in on the "on-beats" the "after-beats," and using the different drums and cymbals for those accents.

Of course, the great Krupa technique, rudimental in origin with a great amount of speed, drama and dynamics, added to his solo style. Revolutionary? In a way, in that he synthesized and expanded on the styles of his early heros Zutty Singleton, Baby Dodds and Chick Webb. In any case, until the beginnings of the be-bop revolution, when any drummer in any dance band took a solo — and because of Gene Krupa almost everyone did in the course of an evenings' program—they sounded like Gene Krupa, though many without his technique, taste, control and theatrical flair. As years went on and Krupa's importance began to come into question, with all the credit being heaped upon drummers like Sidney Catlett and Jo Jones, it should be remembered that solo-wise in those days, even giants like Jones and Catlett sounded like Gene Krupa.

In the Second Band, one is constantly reminded of the Krupa quote, *I certainly have to go along with progress, but it has to be presented carefully and intelligently.* By 1945, Krupa, always a listener, had to be affected by bop music and bop drummers. Though he was relatively quick in grabbing some bop soloists and arrangers for his Second Band, the transition was seemingly harder for Krupa to make. In his Columbia recording in 1945 of the bop-oriented *Leave Us Leap* (still during the string section days), Krupa finally began to incorporate the larger "ride" cymbal for some of his timekeeping efforts, particularly behind the trumpet of Don Fagerquist and the trombone of Leon Cox. However, for most of the ensemble work, and even behind Charlie Ventura's tenor sax solo, the time is kept on the hi-hat, albeit in a looser fashion than in years past, with some "off-the-beat" snare drum accents.

A year later, in Gerry Mulligan's distinctly bopish chart on *How High The Moon* with its "Ornithology" counter-melody, Krupa began to assimilate even more of the characteristics of be-bop drumming, with more ride cymbal use, some left-handed snare drum accents and some "bass-bop" accents on the bass drum ala Max Roach and Kenny Clarke. However, Krupa reverts back to the hi-hat during ensemble passages. In one of Krupa's last commercially recorded charts for Columbia in 1949, George Wallington's *Lemon Drop*, Krupa sounded as "boppish" as he probably ever would. All time is kept in the ride cymbal, there is a lighter overall feel, and the snare drum accents are not as predictable.

The addition of Latin percussionists Ramon Rivera and Hernando Brava helped with the modern flavor. In Krupa's RCA recordings of the following year, there was not much room for modernism of any kind. These were strictly dance sets and novelties done for commercial value only, and since the big-band era was at an end anyway, that was not the time for innovation of any kind. Krupa, who had commented during that period that he felt he had been hurt by some of his leanings to bop in the past, was just trying to keep his band together.

No, Krupa did not make an altogether successful transition to bop drumming. At best, he managed to assimilate some of the characteristics of it — though some rather late in the game — and managed to fit in with most of the more modern arrangements in the book rather well. As a soloist in the Second Band there was some rhythmic evolution and more chances taken, but solo-wise, Krupa perfected and expanded upon what he had initially set down in the Benny Goodman days. This is not to say that Gene Krupa couldn't have made the transition to bop drumming. He had the ears, the technique and he always had a progressive mentality. He could have probably imitated or assimilated the style of anyone he wanted to and that thought probably crossed his mind more than once. He might even have been torn in those years, like Dave Tough was, between "going modern" and/or staying the same. Sure, he could have played like Roach or Clarke, but then he wouldn't be Gene Krupa. And even by 1951, the masses still expected the "Gene Krupa style" from Gene Krupa. What he did, which Teddy Wilson so eloquently describes, was to assimilate those characteristics of modernism which fit into what he already did. In this manner, he would not alienate the old Krupa fans and at the same time, continue to evolve in his own way at his own pace. I give no credence to recent statements by Gerry Mulligan, who is alleged to have said that Krupa had no understanding of the foundations of bop drumming.

Krupa's limitations as a modern drummer, however self-imposed, presented some problems in making the transition to small group playing, which are discussed elsewhere in this work. In the first reincarnation of The Gene Krupa Jazz Trio with Teddy Napoleon and Charlie Ventura, Krupa reverted back, in some ways, to a style he had perfected during the Benny Goodman Trio and Quartet days, with the very heavy bass drum making up for the lack of a bass violin, and the somewhat intricate and amusing (though heavy-handed by critical standards) arrangements designed to keep the masses entertained. Though by this time Krupa was using the ride cymbal almost exclusively for timekeeping chores and had become much more sensitive sound-wise—possibly due to his studies with New York Philharmonic tympanist Saul Goodman—in terms of overall feeling, Krupa sounded more modern in 1947. This is not an indictment by any means.

The Krupa Trio which was designed for mass appeal and bop, by 1951, had lost most of the limited commercial appeal it might have had anyway (though it has of course remained imperative in any jazz soloist's language.) Bop drumming within the Trio would have sounded ridiculous. And again, that wouldn't have been Gene Krupa. Krupa was again at a career crossroads, too, and commercial value had to have priority over innovation.

With Eddie Shu's arrival into the small group fold, initially as a trio and later as a quartet with the addition of English bassist John Drew, the bands took on even more of the characteristics of accepted forms of modernism. If one must put a label on the Krupa groups of the fifties, "mainstream" would be the most accurate. The self-taught and very versatile Shu was basically a Lester Young-influenced reedman who had learned well the licks of bop and cool jazz, and because of his lighter tone and conception brought a lighter feel to the band. And "cool" was "in" during those days, too, so the heavily featured Shu had to have at least satisfied some of the hipsters of the day. With the addition of a bass player, Krupa was finally able to lighten up on the bass drum a bit and use it more for accents, while still keeping it at a steady, though a bit lighter "four." Still, though, much of the music retained the somewhat heavy Krupa feel, with the accents on the snare and bass drums falling into a somewhat predictable—though relatively new for Krupa—pattern. As a drum soloist in those years, there were certain set pieces—like *Sing, Sing, Sing, Stompin' At The Savoy, Flyin' Home*, etc.—which Krupa continued to feature and by and large, had their own set-piece type of solo.

The solo on the most-requested *Drum Boogie*, for instance, was perhaps perfected at a 1952 Jazz at the Philharmonic concert which featured an impressive Krupa pickup trio with Willie Smith on alto saxophone and Hank Jones on piano. It was at this show, later highlighted by the only "recorded live" drum duel with Buddy Rich, that Krupa played the definitive *Drum Boogie* solo, or maybe even the finest solo of his career. The "Boogie" piece represents everything that Krupa was as a soloist, technician, melodist, drummer-for-dancers, dramatist and crowd-pleaser. It begins with the familiar Krupa "dotted-quarter" note pattern of ringing rim-shots on the snare drum, progresses to triplets on the snare and later tom-tom accents almost as if he were going to introduce listeners to every technique one-by-one, builds in volume and complexity to a fever pitch, suddenly drops down to an incredibly soft volume while still continuing the triplet pattern, and finally builds into a shattering climax of a 32nd- note, single-stroke roll replete with more tom-toms and cymbal crashing. And all the while, the bass drum beat "1-2-3-4." And yes, one could dance to it.

This is simply a timeless piece, which can be compared to something along the lines of the Louis Armstrong solo on *West End Blues*, which was virtually perfected at its inception and therefore played that way with only slight variations for years afterward. And to the critics who have said that Krupa fans often "saw what they thought they heard," via the Krupa grimaces, lights and flying hair, the recording of this *Drum Boogie* solo holds up as a classic sans the video portion.

Eddie Wasserman's entrance into the small group helped lighten up the Quartet's approach even more (clarinetist Gale Curtis' tenure was short-lived and not particularly impressive, so it bears no discussion). The Julliard-trained Wasserman had an even lighter and more relaxed conception than Shu—plus he was more studied, more controlled and did double rather successfully on flute—and the Quartet reflected it overall, particularly on some sensitive ballads like *I Can't Get Started* and *September Song*. At the same time some of the more pretentious arrangements of years past were dropped from the book. On production numbers like *Caravan,* the Quartet could almost pass for a modern group. Young modernists like pianists Ronnie Ball and John Bunch, and bassist Jimmy Gannon, helped. And most of the sidemen that played with Krupa during those years quite agree that much of his backing, surprisingly, was rather sensitive.

Ventura's return in 1962 meant even more popularity for the Quartet, what with triumphant tours to Mexico City and Japan. Musically, Krupa always had a tendency to play more heavily behind Ventura as Ventura is, at the least, a heavy reed player. Additionally, Krupa had really begun to slow down. The drum solos were shorter and less demanding, the nightclub engagements were more limited and Ventura was featured on more ballads than ever. Still, the Great New Quartet with Ventura, John Bunch and Knobby Totah on bass was one of Krupa's best. It was relaxed, it swung, it was balanced, and Krupa was, despite his heaviness behind Ventura, perhaps more musical than he ever was, seemingly more concerned with more tonal colors, textures, tonal variety, sensitivity and an increasing use of exploring the tonal capabilities of his cymbals, which now included a large Chinese "swish" to his right. And the ballads gave him more of a chance to perfect his always underrated brushwork, as sensitive and as musical as any drummers' from any era.

Krupa retired in 1967, but came back about two years later with his own groups featuring Eddie Shu back in the reed chair, reunions with Goodman and Chicago-type concerts with the Eddie Condon gang. Krupa's evolution by that time was best exemplified by his "comeback" gig at New York City's Plaza Hotel (Plaza 9 and All That Jazz was the name of the club), where he sounded lighter, more relaxed and more modern than he ever had.

Gene Krupa continued to evolve, however carefully, and whatever was done in the way of progress had to fit in with what comprised his musical beliefs and integrity. Krupa said it best in the introduction to his drum method instruction book published in 1938. *Artistic Drumming,* he said, *comes only with years of varied musical and emotional experiences, and the attainment of success depends largely upon the development of an individual musical personality.* If his assessment was correct, then Gene Krupa was an unqualified success.

THE EARLY YEARS
THROUGH THE
GOODMAN YEARS

CHAPTER TWO

THE EARLY YEARS THROUGH THE GOODMAN YEARS

I *was always the youngest. The baby in our family: two girls and six boys came ahead of me and I was the ninth and final chapter. We originated the generation gap. My oldest sister was 23 years older than me. I was the youngest one of the Chicago jazz gang, too. Well, Benny Goodman beat me by about four months. But before I ever met the Austin High boys — (Eddie) Condon, (Bud) Freeman, Davey Tough and the rest — I was in a kid band at the age of 12. We called ourselves "The Frivolians."*

I started out playing sax. In high school I worked after hours as a soda jerker in a small dance hall. The drummer — and his drums — got me. I used to sneak up when the band was off the stand and try them out. My older brother Pete finally bought me a set of traps. That finished me at high school. The sax and drums — and I flunked out.

I was a chore boy (at age 11 with brother Pete at the Brown Music Company on Chicago's South Side). Did a little bit of everything around the store. Anyway, I wanted into music. Drums just happened to be the cheapest instrument in the wholesale catalogue — $18.00 for a Japanese outfit: large bass drum, snare drum, woodblock, a brass cymbal and a stand. After I made the purchase, I played at every opportunity. The sticks almost never left my hand.

Most of my family hated jazz. And they hated my flunking out even more. They began to put the pressure on, particularly the older ones who were already married and settled down. (They said) "Why doesn't the kid go to work if he doesn't want to go to school, and bring in some money?"

Mama had hoped I would be a priest. She said, "I can understand what music means to you. I want you to do what you want to do. But I want you to have an education, too. I'm sending you to St. Joseph's College. I want you to go down there and give it a real try. Then, if you're still interested in music, you can do it."

Father (Ildefonse) Rapp taught me the appreciation of all music. He was a wonderful trumpet player but strictly legit. But he was marvelously relaxed and cool about all music including jazz. "There are only two kinds of music," he would say, "good and bad." I was at St. Joe's when Condon and the gang were hearing the Rhythm Kings at the Friars and Louis (Armstrong) and Joe (Oliver) at the Lincoln Gardens. I missed all that. Never did hear Oliver and came in later on Louis.

The drive for music was too strong. I returned to Chicago and finished high school there...and spent much of the time sleeping in class. It was tough working jobs at night and getting to school early in the morning.

Suddenly, Davey Tough came to see me. He was leaving the Blue Friars to join the Wolverines. Would I like his place? Would I? I'll level with you: I didn't know that they were picking me not because of any talent, but because they knew I was not on a commercial kick and was young, and they could mold me. Like all the young guys then, they were very much for the real, noncommercial thing.

So I started making the Blue Friars dates. But they were so noncommercial that they would pass up some dates and play others for no dough at all!

Well, you can understand. Maybe they could afford it. I couldn't. I had to get dough. So I began playing with a lot of commercial, or, at least, semi-commercial bands, like the Seattle Harmony Kings, the Hoosier Bell Hops, Joe Kayser, and the Benson Orchestra of Chicago. With these outfits we always managed to get one or two guys who were in our bag, like maybe (Frank) Teschemacher or (Mezz) Mezzrow. But they held the quota down. They were afraid of "hot pollution." And their public was square.

But we kept our connection with the righteous music. Our dates would generally end at around midnight or 1:00 A.M. and we would hightail it to the Three Deuces right opposite the Chicago Theater on State Street. Then we would jam all night. What a gang!

We were so damned cocky! If a guy went with a bread-winning band, he immediately became commercial. Ben Pollack had just brought his new band in from California and was getting started at the Southmoor Hotel. Benny (Goodman) and Jimmy McPartland had joined him. That made them defectors, because Pollack was making money! By our standard — will you believe me? — Pollack was another sweet band like Isham Jones. If McPat or Benny would bring in some other Pollack sidemen to our jams, when they'd go on the stand, we'd walk off, pretending to rest! It was Tesch who was our boy then. He was still poor.

I began hearing drummers Tubby Hall with Carroll Dickerson's Orchestra at the Sunset Cafe and Zutty Singleton with clarinetist Jimmy Noone. They were great! They knew every trick and just how to phrase the parts of the choruses behind the horns, how to lead a man in, what to do at the turn-arounds, when to use sticks and when to use brushes, when to go for the rims or the woodblocks, what cymbals are for.

But there was only one Baby Dodds. He was at Kelly's Stable with his brother Johnny, cornetist Natty Dominique, and a piano player. Baby taught me more than all the others — not only drum playing, but drum philosophy. He did all that the others did, and more. He was the first great drum soloist. His concept went on from keeping time to making the drums a melodic part of jazz. It was partly the way he tuned his drums — the intervals he used. I got that from him. And it was partly his concept of tone. Baby could play a tune on the drums, and if you listened carefully, you could tell the melody!

I kept going back to hear Baby — though sometimes it was a hassle getting into the place because of being underage. Not only was he a great showman, the man played with fantastic drive. Those press rolls! He could really get things moving. It soon became clear how much I admired him, and we struck up a friendship that was only broken by his death in 1959. Until I got to New York a bit later and heard Chick

Webb at the Dunbar Palace, a ballroom in Harlem, Baby was my biggest influence.

The First Record Date December 9, 1927

Billed as McKenzie and Condon's Chicagoans (the former being singer/ kazoo player/successful vaudeville attraction Red McKenzie), we—McPartland (cornet), Teschemacher (saxophone), Joe Sullivan (piano), Condon (guitar), Jim Lanigan (tuba and bass) and I—made four sides: "China Boy," "Sugar," "Nobody's Sweetheart" and "Liza." Musicians really dug them. The New Yorkers, big shots like the Dorseys, Red Nichols, and Bix, felt we had moved music one step ahead by modernizing New Orleans jazz and adding touches of our own.

Bea Palmer, the vaudeville singer, hung out with our gang, and used to come to our sessions at the Deuces. Soon after our record came out—like early 1928—she got a job in New York. She said, "Come on, gang," and we went. No jobs, you understand, but she was flush and helped us raise the train fare. I recall Joe and Tesch going, probably Bud, and Red McKenzie for sure. Jim Lanigan couldn't make it.

We got to New York. Tesch, Condon, Sullivan, Bud Freeman and McPartland were in the band. But the job didn't work out. There we were in the big town with no immediate sources of support. Man, in New York the panic was on.

But there were some boys there who wouldn't let us go hungry...not too hungry. Guys like Bix and Joe Venuti, and Tommy and Jimmy Dorsey. We shacked up at the Cumberland Hotel at 54th and Broadway (later the Bryant). I should say "stacked up," because we were all in one room. One guy registered and the others sneaking in.

We really scuffled it out. Then we began to get a job here and there. Singles, that is. Condon scared up a recording date or two with Fats Waller, and we had a little bread. Then Joe and I got a job, Joe with Red Nichols, and we moved the gang out of the Cumberland sardine can up to the Riverside Towers on Riverside Drive at 79th Street. The towers were so tall and narrow that Condon called them the "Riverside Showers."

With Red Nichols, 1929, as pit drummer on Broadway
in Strike Up The Band/Girl Crazy

I couldn't tell a quarter note from an eighth note and Glenn (trombonist Miller, also in the band) knew it. So every time we got something new to do, I'd pass my part to Glenn who'd hum it for me a few times until I got it in my head and then I'd play it. There must have been 40 men in the band and I'd be drumming away with all my might when Red would signal me to give. I just didn't have the technique to control the drums without killing myself. I was a jazz drummer, not a musician. I used all the Chicago beats, four with one hand and a light press with the other on the second and fourth beats, hand to hand rolls accented and a lot of woodblock rhythms. So, right then and there I resolved to learn the drums technically, from the bottom up. I got myself the best teacher in New York and started in.

About that time, my style began to change. I felt the need to really know my instrument and became deeply involved in studies with Sanford "Gus" Moeller—one of the great drum teachers—while simultaneously learning more and more about jazz by playing and listening in Harlem. I'd practice on the rubber pad six, seven, eight hours during the day. Go out and work. Then, after hours, I'd play uptown...and watch tap dancers and great drummers like George Stafford and Sonny Greer. I learned a lot of rhythmic beats that way.

It was wonderful, exciting period of discovery. By studying, I found it possible to play more gracefully, with control, speed and freedom. By listening and absorbing Chick Webb and a few other cats, I came to realize what could be done in big bands and small.

You had to see and hear Chick to believe it. To begin with, he was a terrific hi-hat man. He could really make those cymbals talk. His sound on the drums was distinctive. Crisp. The way he backed sections, soloists, shaded big band ensembles. And those solos!

When Goodman and Chick had a battle of the bands at the Savoy Ballroom a few years later, I was never cut by a better man. Too bad he died so young. He had so much to offer!

Joining the Russ Columbo Band, 1932

> *Benny organized that band. Jimmy McPartland, Bo Ashford, Harry Goodman, Joe Sullivan, Babe Russin. It was a hell of a good band. We played one season at the Woodmansten Inn in Pelham. Then we played Loews and it was a wonderful experience for me because in each theater we played the pit for the four acts that preceded us and then came up on the stage for our 20 minutes with Russ. We would play the Paradise in New York. They had different conductors each week because Russ couldn't conduct the show, he just led the band on stage. We took pride in the band and he was a fine guy to work for.*

Joining the Benny Goodman Band, March, 1935

> *The band really thrilled me when I heard it on NBC's "Let's Dance" show (which ran for 26 weeks beginning in December, 1934). It was the first time a big band, with jazz as its central interest, played naturally and freely, with that sort of frequency, on coast-to-coast radio.*

Benny Goodman, quoted in Eddie Condon's *Treasury of Jazz*: "The band was shaping up, but the rhythm, especially, wasn't right. Our drummer was merely adequate, and the man I really wanted, Gene Krupa, was in Chicago, playing with Buddy Rogers at the College Inn. John Hammond, the young jazz bug who helped me earlier, went to Chicago to try to corral Krupa. He happened to hit Gene on a night when Rogers, who was versatile but not much of a jazz man, was working out on about 11 different instruments. Gene was having a sad time, but for various reasons he didn't want to change jobs. 'This is going to be a real jazz band,' John urged. 'Think of the kicks, Gene, playing jazz every night.' About then Buddy Rogers picked up another instrument and prepared for a solo. 'I'll come,'" Gene said.

> *I followed Stan King in the Benny Goodman band. I came from the Buddy Rogers band. I knew Stan in the old days when I worked for Red Nichols. The place then was*

Plunkett's (a speakeasy on 53rd Street), and Stan was a very big name then and much respected by me, not so much for his talent, because I was going the other way for guys like Chick Webb and Tommy Miles.

Of course, Benny had a tough time getting started. I remember when we were playing Elitch's Gardens in Denver that we never had more than five people on the floor and it was very discouraging. One night, Benny laid out a lot of rhumbas and stocks. 'What's up Benny?' I said. Benny shook his head. 'I guess this jazz idea of ours is no good. I'm going to get people to dance if I have to play all the mouse music ever written.' I shook my head right back. 'Look Benny, I'm making $85 a week with you and if you're going commercial I might as well go back to Buddy Rogers and make $125 a week. Let's stick to your original idea even if we go under.' Benny did and a week later at the Palomar in Los Angeles, we clicked—for good.

When we opened at the Palomar Ballroom in 1935, all hell broke loose. Had Benny thrown in the towel before his first great triumphs at the Palomar and the Congress in Chicago, there's little doubt but what many of us who have enjoyed success, prominence, and considerable financial reward since the late thirties would ever have attained these heights. Benny built himself a band playing musicians' music, but didn't shoot over the heads of the public. It took the people time, but once they grasped the Goodman musical sermon, they easily understood, accepted, and followed. Being a part of this band was the fulfillment of a dream for any young musician. It allowed us to play the way we honestly wanted to play, with good pay and before huge, appreciative audiences. In the days before the Goodman era, we played that way, too, but in smaller bands with no similar success, or in sessions held in empty halls with no one to appreciate our efforts but the fellows playing the other instruments.

For all that Benny did for music, for jazz, for musicians and for me, I for one, doff my cap in a salute of sincere appreciation.

Musically speaking, to state that the period I spent playing drums in Benny Goodman's orchestra was about the happiest of my career, would be a gross understatement. I doubt if mere words can sum up or begin to express the inward sense of enjoyment derived from playing with the great organization that Benny built and which he supervised in that quiet manner and (with) fine taste.

After the record-breaking engagement at New York's Paramount Theater (March, 1937), it got so we never had any time. Rehearsals, jobs, traveling, personal life became a jumble. Sleep was a rarity. It seemed we were playing all the time, sometimes doubling and tripling jobs. At one point, we were doing a radio show, the Paramount Theater and the Hotel Pennsylvania, all at once. I guess one of the reasons the band got so good was because we never stopped playing.

Tell you one thing, Benny and I worked particularly well together. And still do. Often something almost magical happens as we play. He feeds me and, in turn, I feed him, and the excitement builds. Working with him always is a great experience. Of course we've had out disputes. But the relationship has remained firm over the years. The only thing I'm unhappy about is that I didn't have his business acumen — because Benny, along with being a great musician, knows what the score is commercially.

PRIMARY SOURCES

1)Rudi Blesh, Combo: U.S.A.

2)Krupa interview with Burt Korall, **International Musician,** September, 1972.

3)Krupa interview in Benny Goodman Tribute, **down beat Magazine,** January 12, 1951.

4)Krupa comments in Gene Krupa Tribute issue, **Modern Drummer Magazine,** October-November, 1979.

5)Notes to *That Drummer's Band* (Epic).

Gene Krupa

THE GOODMAN
BREAKUP AND THE
RECONCILIATION

CHAPTER THREE

THE GOODMAN BREAKUP

Gene Krupa was, perhaps, the first bonafide "star" to emerge from the swing era. Of course, that had little to do with pure musicianship, but nevertheless, Gene Krupa had what his employer, Benny Goodman, didn't: movie star looks, natural flamboyance, and an obvious—though sincere—flair for visual showmanship. Within the Goodman organization, Krupa became the idol of the bobby-sox/jitterbug contingent. Complicating matters was the fact that however popular, Krupa was still a sideman, though he was a sideman rapidly commanding more attention than the leader.

Benny Goodman has never relished sharing the spotlight with anyone, if one is to believe in the accuracy of statements over the years from the likes of former Goodman sidemen/co-stars Anita O'Day, Zoot Sims, Jess Stacy, etc. There are, indeed, hundreds of "Benny stories." The prime example of this Goodman quirk was best demonstrated in the disastrous 1953 "Goodman Revival Band"/Louis Armstrong tour, when Goodman pulled out after only five shows due to his alleged dissatisfaction at having to share the stage with Armstrong. As Goodman was heard to remark to John Hammond, "We don't need Louis Armstrong. The attraction is the revival of the old Goodman Band." Krupa, a featured sideman on this tour, took over leadership and master of ceremonies duties after Goodman departed.

Certainly, part of the 1938 rift had to do with Goodman's disturbance at Krupa's increasing popularity. But matters seemed to be coming to a musical head as well. Toward the end of 1937, airshots of the Goodman Band reveal that Krupa's drumming was becoming increasingly unsubtle, almost as if his desire was to be featured on every tune. Krupa's rather boisterous showing at the January, 1938, Carnegie Hall Concert is a perfect illustration. Goodman could not have been thrilled. Krupa cannot be entirely faulted, however. He was but 29 years old at this time, was subject not only to screaming adulation but more and more sales and pep talks from the promoters and booking agencies. Surely, they had their own best interests at heart, but their probable message to Gene Krupa was that he couldn't lose as the leader of his own outfit.

Those who attended some of the shows during the one-week Goodman engagement at Philadelphia's Earle Theater (February 26 - March 3, 1938) claim that the leader and Krupa were openly feuding on stage. The crowds were screaming for Gene to "go" from the moment the band hit the stage. Krupa responded with some bits of gesturing directed toward Goodman, obviously meaning, "I'm not allowed." The audience booed, and whenever Krupa did a solo bit, Goodman seemed to go out of his way to appear half asleep.

Gene Krupa quit on March 3. It was a resignation that shocked the world of music. Less than six weeks later, Gene Krupa staffed, rehearsed and opened with his own swing band. Goodman hired Dave Tough for the drum chair and didn't personally reconcile with Krupa until weeks later. And reconciliation was initiated by Krupa. There were various and sundry outbursts, however minor, between Gene and BG until Gene's passing.

Metronome Magazine/March, 1938

"I'd Sure Like My Own Band" — Krupa
But, Despite Rumors, Gene Won't Leave
Goodman Gang For Quite A While, States
Official Report. . .But Then?

The rumor that Gene Krupa is going to leave Benny Goodman and start his own band flows more freely than ever though dance bandom's main arteries in New York. And, what's more, it's not being denied!

From an impeccable source comes the report that such an action on Gene's part is quite possible, though not entirely probable. The Mad Man of the Drums has always harbored a keen desire to front his own outfit, but for various reasons, among them his unfailing loyalty to King Benny, has never gone through with the idea.

However, recently the question once more came to a head. Said Benny to Krupa: "Gene, I certainly don't want to stand in your way one bit — if you feel like starting your own band, go to it, and the best of luck to you!"

Said Goodman's managers to Gene: "We'll be behind you one hundred percent, and we'll do everything in our power to make you a great success. However, we advise you to wait a while (perhaps a year) before you jump off the big end. It's going to be a deep plunge, and you want to make certain first that you're ready to come up once you dive in!"

Said Gene to himself: "Guess I'll wait awhile — but shucks, I'd sure like to have my own band!"

And so the matter stands today. Chances are you'll be hearing all sorts of rumors that Gene is planning to leave Benny tomorrow or the day after. The chances are even greater, for a while at least, that he'll be on Benny's stand for a while to come. And the chances are greatest of all that once Gene does leave Goodman to start his own band, Dave Tough, the greatest scribbling drummer and drumming scribbler dance bandom has ever known, will become a permanent fixture with the Goodman emporium.

But all that won't happen tomorrow!

Metronome Magazine/March, 1938

"We're Pals!" - Benny
And Gene - But?

Official Statements Deny Ill Feelings,
But
Benny And Krupa Keep Apart After
Admitting Initial Flare-up

Here are two official statements:

From Benjamin Goodman: "There's nothing wrong between Gene and me. He wanted to have his own band, and so I let him go. I wish him the best of luck."

From Eugene Krupa: "There's nothing wrong between Benny and me. We didn't always agree on all angles of music, and, what's more, I've always wanted to have my own band. I think Benny will always have a great band."

And so, from these two very conciliatory statements, it appears that Benny Goodman and Gene Krupa are still the best of friends, despite the fact that, instead of playing for Benny, Gene is leading a rival band. **Metronome** does not advocate emphasizing trouble — on the other hand, **Metronome** does advocate authenticity. In that light, note the following facts:

1. Benny Goodman and Gene Krupa have never been seen together since their split.

2. Benny Goodman has not appeared at any of Gene Krupa's band rehearsals.

3. Gene Krupa has not appeared in the Manhattan Room of the Pennsylvania Hotel since he and Benny split.

4. Benny Goodman acts happier than he has at any time since he started his band.

5. Benny Goodman is now easily the greatest personal attraction within his own orchestra.

6. The style of the Goodman band has changed greatly since the departure of Krupa.

7. Krupa has appeared as a guest artist on numerous radio shows, including Tommy Dorsey's twice — but never on the Goodman Show.

8. Victor, to whom Krupa was signed for two years, and for whom Goodman records, permitted Krupa to record for Brunswick.

9. Jim Mundy immediately stopped arranging for Goodman and started to arrange for Krupa.

Those are conditions exactly as they exist: they are not "official statements." Draw you own conclusions.

If you have decided that nothing is wrong between Benny and Gene, you can stop reading now.

But to those of you who have decided that there is something wrong, more definite hints as to direct causes are due you. Again, you are invited to draw your own conclusions:

1. Goodman let Krupa go without a murmur, despite the fact that legally he had him tied to an expensive contract that had quite some time to run.

2. Krupa, receiving about five hundred dollars per week from Goodman, was quite willing to forego that income in favor of the insecurity that necessarily befalls a new band leader.

3. Krupa was continually drawing more plaudits than any other man within the Goodman organization.

4. Benny spends much of his spare time listening to chamber music.

5. Gene spends much of his spare time listening to jungle music.

6. Benny lives for his clarinet.

7. Gene lives for his drums.

8. Both sides readily admit a flare-up in a Philadelphia Theater (The Earle).

9. Krupa left the week after the flare-up — **without giving or being asked to give two week's notice.**

From all of which, it must be plenty obvious by this time to all of you, that despite the tact and diplomacy that both Mr. Goodman and Mr. Krupa have used in their official statements, the relationship between the two is by no means as amicable as it was. It's too bad, too, because for years Benny and Gene had been very close friends and mutual admirers. They played in many bands together before Benny organized his own and asked Gene to come with him. After that they were huge successes together. Now, chances are, they'll both continue to be huge successes — but not together as very close friends, and possibly not even as mutual admirers.

Looked at from a social point of view, all this is too bad. Looked at from a musical point of view, it may all be to the good.

THE GOODMAN RECONCILIATION/1938

Metronome Magazine/June, 1938

**Benny And Gene
Kiss And Make Up**

Budding Feud Nipped As Goodman Gang Visits Krupa Killers In Philly Cafe, Then Copy Ballgame...Move May End Goodman-Dorsey Tiff

The King and the Crown Prince are reconciled! In a dramatic setting on Friday, the thirteenth of May, within the confines of Philadelphia's Arcadia Restaurant, Benny Goodman and Gene Krupa clasped hands and officially ended what was commencing to turn into the most bitter feud in the history of dance bandom.

It was entirely impromptu — as such events should be. Krupa's Killers were playing at the Arcadia. Goodman's Gang was doing a one-nighter in Philly which ended early, at 12:30 (a.m.), Gene sent an emissary to Benny's Boys, inviting all of them to come to the restaurant as his guests. The majority, including the King, accepted, and entered the Arcadia just as the last floor-show was going on.

Gene, acting as emcee, spied his guests as they entered, and in short order publicly and warmly welcomed Benny. Goodman responded by coming out on the floor, and in an unpretentious and since-sounding speech, personally wished Krupa and his band all the luck in the world. And then, just to make the affair more personal and sincere, Benny and Gene retired by themselves to the bar, where, so far as could be gleaned from supposedly causal but very interested glances, all differences were forgotten.

Benny, upon returning to New York, told **Metronome**: "Gene's a fine guy and he's got a great band — give him a few months more and it'll be even greater than it is now!"

Gene, when contacted via long-distance phone, was even more ejaculatory. *Everything's fine*, he exclaimed. *I knew a lot of people were making too much fuss about nothing. It was swell of Benny to come down to the place to see us. Naw, there's absolutely nothing wrong at all. Why they even licked us in baseball on Sunday. It was close: only 19 to 7. Benny's one great guy*!

The Goodman-Krupa reconciliation is a happy happening for dance bandom. Before it occurred, a little battle was brewing between two rival factions with Benny facing a possible line-up of Tommy Dorsey, Krupa, and even Jimmy Dorsey.

It's an obvious conclusion that Tommy never did relish Goodman's having captured both Dave Tough and Bud Freeman, even though he's now much more than satisfied with Hymie Schertzer and his new sax section. Even when the two men were both living in the Pennsylvania Hotel a month or so ago, they were never seen together, a rather surprising observation when one realizes how close they were in days of yore. Rumors around town persist that Dorsey is contemplating a counter-raid on Goodman's Gang, with (pianist) Jess Stacy the first focal point, though official confirmation of such an attack has never been issued.

The entire situation has been unhealthy. There's been much tension between the bands and apparently no one has felt like being the first one to relieve it. But men like Goodman, Dorsey and Krupa are too big to permit apparently petty squabbles to blossom into bitter feuds, as they almost always do when left to bloom by themselves. In the interests of the dance music business in general, as well as for their own personal satisfaction, the leaders should get together and work out their differences, instead of just shutting up like clams and casting dirty looks.

The Goodman-Krupa kiss-and-make-up-get-together is the first break. There's no apparent reason why before long there shouldn't be a case of three-part harmony existing once again. When that happens, the late combatants can be called "big-time" men as well as "big-time" leaders.

THE

FIRST BANDS

1938–1943

CHAPTER FOUR

THE REVIEWS OF THE FIRST BANDS, 1938-1943

George T. Simon
Metronome
Magazine
May, 1938

In the neighborhood of four thousand neighborhood and visiting cats scratched and clawed for points of vantage in the Marine Ballroom of Atlantic City's Steel Pier on Saturday, April 16, and then, once perched on their pet posts, proceeded to welcome with most exuberant howls and huzzahs the first public appearance of drummer-man Gene Krupa and his newly-formed jazz band. The way the felinic herd received, reacted to, and withstood the powerful onslaughts of Krupa's quadruple "f" musical attacks left little doubt that Gene is now firmly entrenched at the helm of a new swing outfit that's bound to be recognized very shortly as one of the most potent bits of catnip ever to be fed to the purring public that generally passes as America's swing contingent.

If Gene had any cause for worry, that cause was completely submerged before his band's musical history was even one set old. Right from the opening strains of his theme (*Apurksody* — read the first five letters backwards) and on through the colossal arrangement of *Grandfather's Clock*, which officially opened proceedings, it was as obvious as the hair that had already fallen into Gene's face that his band would satisfy the most belligerent cat's meow. Throughout the evening the kids and the kittens shagged, trucked, jumped up and down and down and up, and often yelled and screamed at the series of solid killer-dillers that burst forth from the instruments of the Men of Krupa. When proceedings started, they were lined 45 deep around the huge bandstand, and when at 1:30 (a.m.) the band led its limp lips and limbs from the field of battle, at least one-third of that number of rows remained in an upright position—as thrilling a tribute as any opening band leader could possibly hope for.

Krupa's band is a loud edition of what Goodman's Gang used to be, pulling its punches even less and presenting for the most part a solid, two-fisted A.C. attack that varies more in tempo than it does in volume of intense drive. Paced by a powerful six-man brass section, it maintains a pace that at times is almost punishing in its fierceness, in the way it pelts your ears, and leaves them ringing, and even more so in its ability to hold your musical interest while varying little in musical format.

Of course, the very fact that Gene's Genesis was something new made its first public appearance exceedingly exciting. That, and Gene's remarkably sincere showmanship, were the motivating forces that first caused the assembled cats to howl with glee. But it took a good deal more to keep them purring for the rest of the long evening, and it's in the purring department, in its ability to sustain interest, that the young band really exhibited its true merits.

The merits consisted of, in the first place, 60 or so great arrangements supplied by Jimmy Mundy, Chappie Willett, Fletcher Henderson, Dave Schulze, George Siravo, and a few other members of the band. Then there was a truly remarkable brass sextet that had colossal drive, fine intonation, and a brilliant ensemble attack. The rhythm section, paced by Gene and a great bassist named Horace Rollins, kept swinging out all night at a remarkably steady pace and all the time doing much to propel the other sections as well as the hot soloists right out into very high and elated space.

Of those soloists, four stood out especially so far. On tenor sax, Vido Musso blew forth a tone and licks that were even improvements over what he used to play with Goodman—which is probably enough praise in itself. On trombone, Bruce Squires, though still exhibiting a tendency to overdo his lip trills, really emitted some rhythmic, almost gut-bucket riffs that stamp him as one of the few slip-horn artists today who played an effective hot style on that instrument.

However, the two hot trumpeters, Tommy Gonsoulin and Dave Schulze, really supplied the most exciting hot passages of the night. The former is a high-note screecher whose blunt, remarkably consistent "hit-'em-on-the-nose" attack has a telling effect. The latter is a bit more subtle: his choice of prettier phrases played with a magnificent, ringing tone, comprise the most thrilling bit of soloing within the entire Krupa entourage.

The third trumpeter in the section, Tommy (Tummy) diCarlos, is also a remarkable musician who combines a marvelous intonation and attack with as brilliant and piercing tone as has been heard in these parts since Charlie Spivak left for Chicago. And the remaining members of the brass section, trombonists Chuck Evans and Charles McCamish, deserve much commendation, if only because they round out a fine brass sextet. The latter also plays some good hot passages.

Looking at the performance from a purely musical point of view (which is what you're doing now), the band did fall down in one section, and that was the saxes. True, the acoustics within the shell of the Marine Ballroom have always been tough, but compared with the rhythm and the brass, the reed men were definitely the weak sisters of the evening. Their phrasing at times was very good, but for a white group, their intonation was far below par, and their work as an ensemble unit often very sloppy. Gene has a good leadman in Murray (Jumbo) Williams, and the other men also possess good tones, but some more serious rehearsing and cooperation on individual conceptions of pitch are very much in order. The causes for the band's rough spots, that many critics during the course of the opening evening excused, as ascribed to the short time which the band has played together, can be traced directly to laxity — on the part of the sax section alone.

However, what could be excused, and ascribed to the short time, was the singing of Jerry Kruger, the tall showgirlish lass who joined before the opening. Fine things can be expected from her, but on the opening night she was overcome by 1) the excusable lack of knowledge concerning her material, and 2) the less excusable and apparently insatiable desire to sing everything in the style of Billie Holiday. More time and originality will help Miss Kruger a lot, for she has the basic stuff.

Time, of course, is going to help Krupa's band a lot too — that is, from a musical aspect. From a commercial point of view, the band already has just about everything:

colossal drive and swing, marvelous Krupa showmanship, some novelties in which the entire band plays tom-toms attached to the attractive music stand; all in all, an approach to the younger and shaggier dancing element that, with Krupa's aid, has proved so successful to the Goodman Gang, and which, even without the aid of the Gang, will quite conceivably help Krupa's band to become a huge financial and social success.

. . .The band played an afternoon session first, and Gene was so nervous that he almost buried his head in drum music which he probably knew cold. The height of magnanimity and sincerity were exhibited by Mr. Krupa and Miss Kruger, who good-naturedly and graciously signed autographs all night long—dance bandom could stand more personalities like that...Probably the most excited person in the place was Ethel Krupa, Gene's attractive wife, who just kept on smiling and beaming all night long. Quite a few music-world celebrities came down for the opening—Willard Alexander of MCA, Mike Nidorf of Rockwell-O'Keefe (!), Joe Higgins of Brunswick, Abe Olman of Irving Berlin, and, of course, Dorsey-Berigan-Krupa managers Arthur Michaud and John Gluskin.

Burt Korall
International Musician
September, 1972

The G K Orchestra, a showcase for its leader at the outset, was an immediate success. After the first year, however, it became apparent to the young leader that he would have to diversify to retain the band's high level of appeal. The drummer man increasingly shared the spotlight with his singers and soloists.

Gene Krupa
International Musician
September, 1972

That change in direction helped us make it. Singers like Leo Watson, Irene Daye and Anita O'Day, and our soloists, particularly Roy Eldridge, were what put the band over. Sure people came to see me. But Anita and Roy and the others gave us that extra push and got things cooking.

Leonard Feather
Metronome Magazine
May, 1943

Gene Krupa's Orchestra was five years old on April 17. Much water has flowed under the bridge, and much hair has been added to Remo Biondi's mustache, since those pioneer days. Remo is the sole surviving sideman. But the band still plays quite a few of the earliest arrangements, such as *Blue Rhythm Fantasy* and *Wire Brush Stomp.*"

The way personnels are shuffling around nowadays, it's only fair to judge a band by the material it has in the books rather than by the way it happens to play that material on any one given night. For instance, when Gene opened in Newark (The Terrace Room) he had just finished seven weeks of theaters: there were six men in the band who had joined during that period and consequently didn't know any of the arrangements, except the few he had been using in the stage show.

Considering, then, that there was so much sight-reading going on, the band sounded remarkably good at Newark. The trumpet section is truly a powerful quartet. The reeds are excellently led by Johnny Bothwell, who is also a good solo man. The rhythm section is one of the best around, as might well be expected with such a great drummer at its foundation.

Make no mistake, Gene hasn't forsaken solidity for showmanship. He still remembers that a drummer's main function is to set a fine beat, underline rhythmic effects and phrases in the arrangement, and generally provide a good foundation. Naturally, being a drummer-leader and an idol of the jitterbugs, he also has to take an inordinate number of solos. I am still dead set against drum solos in any way, shape, manner or form, because I believe melody is an essential part of all real jazz. However, if you must have drum solos, they might as well by Krupa's for his technique is still a wondrous thing.

Since there must be some limit to the number of solos a leader can take when he happens to be a drummer, the role of soloist-in-chief is rightly assigned to someone else, and the person very logically chosen is Roy Eldridge.

A cornerstone in the Krupa band for two years now, Roy is as indispensable as Gene himself. Broadly speaking, every number in the books either has an Eldridge solo or no solo at all. Roy plays in the section, he plays instrumental specialties, he takes semi-straight solos on ballads, and he sings such jive tunes as *Big Fat Mama* and *Knock Me A Kiss* in a manner so disarmingly charming that you overlook his lack of a voice. And Roy even plays drums on some of the ballads when Gene is out front conducting. Good drums, too.

Roy is one musician who often sounds better in a big band, playing arrangements, than he does at jam sessions. When he's jamming with no holds barred, his ideas are apt to grow a little too frantic at times; when he's doing his sweet-but-hot chorus on *Embraceable You* with Krupa, the ideas are controlled and better formulated, still displaying that unique semi-dirty tone and harmonically imaginative style that have made him one of the all-time greats of the trumpet.

There are good soloists in the band. Buddy DeFranco, who got his start with a Tommy Dorsey amateur contest in Philly, plays some really exciting Goodmanesque clarinet, also does some you-take-four-and-I'll-take-four choruses on alto, playing against Charlie Ventura, who's a smooth, Chu(Berry)-toned tenor man with plenty of truly remarkable individual solo spots in such tunes as *Out of Nowhere*.

Dodo Marmorosa, a new star from Pittsburgh, is a highly promising pianist in the single-note style. It's good to know he'll be around at least a few months more (he's 17).

Gloria Van is the most glorious thing these eyes have seen next to a microphone in years. Vocally, she's no Anita O'Day, but then who is? Anita's departure left a sad gap in the band. Gene Howard is a good enough ballad-purveyor with an easy manner and voice.

The arrangements are currently being handled partly by an under- publicized young man named Bert Ross, who made the now famous arrangement for Benny Goodman of *Why Don't You Do Right?* (He also made *Rhumboogie* for Will Bradley, and spent the last eight months with Scat Davis.) Examples of his work for Krupa include *Nevada*, *As Time Goes By*, and *Right Kind of Love*. There are also a few arrangements by Toots Camarata and Jimmy Mundy. Elton Hill, the band's staff scorer for several years, is now busy in a defense plant; Sam Musiker, ex-Krupa clarinetist, has sent in such arrangements as *Clair de Lune* from Stuart Airfield. Add to this the mixture of older stuff by Fred Norman, Chappie Willett, Remo Biondi et al., and you have a library that varies in quality but is good on the whole.

In sum, Gene's band today rates #1 commercially because of the leader's name and personality plus the general musical standards; it rates B Plus artistically, mainly because of Roy Eldridge and a couple of other soloists, plus the general musical standards. It's a band which, in view of the shifting sands on which today's band personnels are finding themselves, does credit to the leader and his men.

GENE KRUPA ON THE FIRST BAND'S ARRANGEMENTS

One More Dream,
composer unknown.
Recorded 4/14/38

This comes from my first session as a bandleader. Helen Ward, another Benny Goodman graduate, sings this one, very much as she sang with the Old Man. The band plays with a Goodman-Fletcher Henderson influence; easy and relaxed.

Rhythm Jam,
composed and ar-
ranged by Chappie
Willett.
Recorded 6/19/38

Chappie Willett was my first arranger and we got some great things from him—"Blue Rhythm Fantasy," "I Know That You Know," "Grandfather's Clock." Vido Musso of the tenor sax with the big sound and lots of drive is featured on this one. Vido loved to have the band play loud and hard behind him, and we certainly obliged. To get back to Chappie again, I'll never forget how much he did for bands that had to play shows; invariably vaudeville acts brought in music that was worse to listen to than to play, and it was murder to play from those sad, cut- up, marked-up, beat-up stocks. Chappie had the knack of being able to put down on paper what the performer wanted, and yet make it sound good.

Tutti Frutti,
composed by
Fisher-Gaillard.
Recorded 8/10/38

The changes in this thing are kind of boppish. And this was one of the first scat-singing choruses on record. Listen to that Leo (Watson)—what a wild cat! I always dug him, all the way back when he was working in a group called "Ben Bernie's Nephews"—what a crazy name for them!—in the College Inn of the Hotel Sherman in Chicago. Then they became the "Six Spirits of Rhythm." Whenever I ran into them I used to sit in. I dug Leo and his chittlin' trombone and the way he played drums too. What a showman—gee whiz! And he was so happy all the time. He couldn't get enough out of life. What's that he told you? "Everyday was like his birthday to him?" That's just the way he was.

Apurksody (**Theme**), composed by Gene Krupa and Chappie Willett. Recorded 12/12/38

We kind of goofed around till we found what we thought told the feel of the band. We didn't want to sound too much like Goodman, but still we wanted to swing. Ellington was really more of an influence, I'd say. We recorded this at the same time we made that "Some Like It Hot" picture (1938) out in Hollywood. Hey, that's Sam Donahue on tenor. I'd recognize Sam's playing any place. This sounds nice and clean, doesn't it? That reminds me of something that happened when we played this at the Paramount Theater in New York. There was this trumpeter we had—Ray something-or-other—and he was what you'd call one of these dressing-room guys. He'd be up there practicing all the time and hitting those high Z's. Well, one night the entire Paul Whiteman band came in to catch the show and naturally I wanted to do good. But our first trumpeter took sick, and this Ray fellow told me, "Don't worry, Gene, I got it covered." So we go on stage and comes the theme, and, man, I tell you, this guy hasn't played the right note yet. It was awful. Poor guy, as soon as we finish the show he dashes off the stage, but for some reason or other the elevator that was supposed to take us up to our dressing room wasn't working. So what does he do but run eight flights up the stairs to his dressing room, and by the time we get up there, he's back at it again, hitting all those high Z's like nothing at all happened.

Quiet and Roll 'Em, composed by Krupa-Donahue-Biondi-Richards. Arranged by Chappie Willett. Recorded 2/26/39

We got the title from the direction they used to give us on the movie lot, just before they'd begin to shoot. That's Donahue's tune and arrangement (discographers list Willett as arranger.) *You know, Sam had a lot of charm to his playing; he had almost a kind of Lester Young sound, and he'd play pretty things and interesting changes and he always had such a good time. I'm so glad he's doing well these days. He's such a gentleman. That clarinet is by the other Sam - Sam Musiker. Listen to that good pure sound he used to get.*

Sweetheart, Honey, Darlin,' Dear, composed by Biondi-Krupa. Arranged by Ray Biondi. Recorded 7/24/39

It was funny how some of the things we finally recorded first got their start. I remember one night when we were playing the Sunnybrook Ballroom in Pottstown, Pennsylvania, and Ray Biondi passed out the parts for a simple riff he'd conceived. It wasn't an arrangement then—just a few lines and chord indications. The guys jammed it and tried to get something going and then Leo Watson said, "Hey, let me get in on this." So he made up the title and it fit really good.

Later on Irene started singing it, and we got some more words, and this is it. I still think this is one of the best things Irene ever did; in fact, the band plays with a lot of spirit, too, wouldn't you say?

Symphony in Riffs, composed and arranged by Benny Carter. Recorded 9/20/39

Benny Carter was always ahead of his time — this arrangement, I'm sure, was written at least three or four years before we recorded it, but just listen to it! And the band is tight and precise, and yet loose enough so that it swings. The late Corky Cornelius on trumpet and Sam Donahue on tenor sax have excellent solos on this one.

Drummin' Man, composed by Parham-Krupa. Arranged by Fred Norman. Recorded 11/2/39

That was the title they hung on me at the time. We still get requests for it. That's Corky (Cornelius) on trumpet. I guess you'd call him the first of the screamers. Remember that he was left-handed? People used to stop and stare at him because he looked different when he played, but most of them never could figure out what it was. Listen to Irene (Daye). You know, I'd say Rosemary Clooney based her style on Irene's. She has real good diction; you can understand every word. My solo? Notice how I stop every phrase on the last beat of the bar. In those days it was considered a cardinal sin to carry over and end on the first beat of the next bar. But now all the drummers do it to bring in the rest of the band.

Tuxedo Junction, composed by Feyne-Hawkins-Johnson. Arranged by Elton Hill. Recorded 5/8/40

This was strictly a cover version for Erskine Hawkins' big hit on this tune. That's Corky on trumpet and Ray Biondi playing single-string guitar. He has sort of that Blind Lemon (Jefferson) feel. Ray did a lot of things for the band. He played and he composed and arranged and he was my right-hand man for years. He didn't arrange this, though. Elton Hill did. We made it in Liederkranz Hall, and it was big, and a great relief for the band because before this we'd always had to record in a small studios with lots of padding. Notice one thing, though. There's absolutely no presence at all on the drums. I guess that's because in those small studio they used to have to keep down the sound of the drums; they hadn't developed the technique of miking the drums to get some presence, the way they do today.

Drum Boogie,
composed by
Eldridge-Krupa.
Arranged by Elton
Hill.
Recorded 1/17/41

Roy Eldridge gave this to us before he ever joined the band. I used to go to hear him all the time at the Capitol Lounge in Chicago — it was right next to the stage door of the Chicago Theater — and Roy used to play this thing, only he called it "Rare Back." I told him I liked it, so he said I could have it. Those were the days when every band was on a boogie-woogie kick, so we called it Drum Boogie. It turned out to be our most requested number through the years. I remember every time we'd come back to the Paramount Theater, I always thought I'd come in with something in place of "Drum Boogie." And then after the show Bob Weitmann, the manager, would come backstage and shake his head and say, "Well, Gene, now are you convinced we should have "Drum Boogie?" And so we'd put it back in. That's Clint Neagley on alto and Shorty Sherock on trumpet. Shorty came from Gary, Indiana, which was close enough to sound like a Chicago boy. Hey, listen to the way I stop that break right on the fourth beat of the bar again. I stop completely, and then I make the final chorus.

Let Me Off Uptown,
composed by
Evans-Bostic.
Recorded 5/8/41

You say the tempo's slower than you're used to hearing it? I guess it is. But, you know, it's a funny thing about tempos. After you've played a number many times, it seems you almost automatically increase the tempo. Maybe it's because, subconsciously, you feel you need to give it some added excitement, and you can't think of another way to do it. But you can work it another way, too — you can slow down a tune purposely, just to get it into a different groove. I remember when I was with Goodman, and Benny was off the stand and it was up to me to set the tempos. I used to try some that were different from those he used to set — some faster and some slower — hoping the guys might get a fresh approach. It worked many times, but there were some times when I goofed pretty badly, too. On this particular recording we had the feeling pretty well set because we'd been playing it on the job for quite some time before we recorded it. You know that part where the crowd roars? We felt we had to put that on the record — even though it's only the guys in the band yelling — because almost every time we played the tune, the crowd actually did roar in that spot.

After You've Gone, composed by Creamer-Layton. Recorded 6/5/41

That's Sam Musiker on clarinet; he sounds a lot like Barney Bigard on this one. Hey, listen to that tempo. I couldn't play that fast today anymore.

Rockin Chair, composed by Hoagy Carmichael. Recorded 7/2/41

I remember this date well: it was a rough one. It was while we were playing at the Pennsylvania Hotel, and we had to make quite a few takes of this number. You can imagine how hard it was on Roy's chops. But what finally came out I think is pretty sensational. To show you the kind of conscientious guy Roy was, we played the tune that night again on the job at the hotel, and this time Roy missed the ending. I looked at him, and I could see big tears in his eyes, I could also see his lip. It looked like a hamburger! If this isn't the greatest Roy Eldridge on record, it's awfully close. "Little Jazz" plays with intense feeling and splendid execution — he always did. It was a pleasure to be associated with him musically.

Violets for yourFurs, composed by Matt Dennis Recorded 10/3/41

Johnny Desmond came into my band, replacing Howard Dulaney. He stayed until he was inducted into the Army, where Glenn Miller grabbed him for his Air Force band, and the rest is history. Johnny was a smash in London, and of course he's a big star here today. He gives a nice easy performance in this number, proving once again that most great vocalists gained invaluable knowledge and experience kicking around with bands.

Bolero at the Savoy, composed by Krupa-Biondi-Mundy-Carpenter. Arranged by Elton Hill. Recorded 11/25/41

This was Ray Biondi's and my answer to all those dance teams that used to give us their arrangements of Ravel's "Bolero" to play. They always did it in 4/4 time but, as you know, Ravel wrote it in 3/4. Notice that we have a six-bar intro which gives it a 3/4 time feeling right away. Charlie Carpenter, a fellow many of us remember from the Savoy Ballroom days, wrote the lyrics for us.

That's What You Think, composed by Werner and Werner. Recorded 2/26/42

Maybe you don't know it, but I've always been a Ravel fan. Well, for a long time I kept looking for a good piece with lyrics, and then one day these two girls, Kay and Sue Werner, came in with this. I love what Anita does with it. You can hear how much she sounds like a jazz horn.

Knock Me A Kiss,
composed by Jackson.
Recorded 4/2/42

This used to be a great vehicle for us in theatres. Roy (vocalist on this track) would break up every show with it. And you know, as a singer he was pretty great too. Hey, listen to the band; it's got a fine feeling too, doesn't it?

Massachusetts,
composed by Razaf-Roberts. Arranged by Elton Hill.
Recorded 7/13/42

I like that feeling! This is one of the best things she's (vocalist Anita O'Day) ever done. Jeez, but the band sounds good on this one! (Elton Hill) was a one-time trumpet player turned arranger and he always seemed to write just the right sort of things that guys would like to play. I know the trumpets sound especially good here, and we had a great section at that time, but if Elton hadn't written so right for them — well, they wouldn't have sounded like this.

THE

DRUG BUST:

SUMMER, 1943

CHAPTER FIVE

THE DRUG BUST: SUMMER, 1943

I *was caught because I had fired my valet. He put some "tea" in my topcoat in my dressing room, and the Feds saw him do it. They were always hanging around the bands waiting for one of us to cough. They waited until I went to the hotel and then moved in. I think I made a mistake by hiring a big lawyer. The papers played it up big, and I became a political football.*

What happened was that the District Attorney was coming up for reelection and I was just what he needed. Possession was one thing—bad enough, all right. But this teenage kid, a fan, had offered to help me until I got a new valet. He carried my coat to the hotel, so the D.A. had this big thing: using a minor to transport dope. And I didn't even know it was in my coat!

I had 94 days. My appeal did not come up until a year and a half later. They brought the valet in again to testify. He had cooled off during the 18 months, recanted what he had said, and cleared me of even knowing that the tea was in my coat. The judge cleared me of any charges.

I felt pretty bad. I didn't want to see anybody. I came home here. I had just built this house in 1940, I think, and this thing happened in 1943. I came back here and I was going to go into writing music and so forth. Maybe teaching and stuff like that. And Benny Goodman called me up one day and said, "Come on out to the house and we'll play some." So I did, and it felt good and he talked me into going in the New Yorker Hotel with him. I did, and I saw that the people accepted what I had to offer. In other words, "Come home honey, all is forgiven."

I'd broken down the nightclub scene, but I was a little apprehensive about the theater scene. That's something else. I used to see people parading up and down, saying, "Don't go see this guy. He smoked a stick of tea." So I went into the Paramount Theater with Tommy Dorsey and was received there, too. I stayed with Tommy about six, seven months, then formed my own band and started up again.

They asked a lot of questions: "How does it feel, and what does it do for you, does it make you play better?" But I can only tell you about one part of the scene and that's the marijuana scene, which I was very much involved in, and all I could tell them was, I don't think I was exactly a failure, but on the other hand, I think I could have been a lot more successful in the field. For instance, I just couldn't see doing a cigarette commercial, could you? Not with the stigma I had, don't you see?

I tell the kids about this, and I tell them about my experiences. Another direction that I go into is that it makes you kind of stupid. Take a look at me. It does. Really. It slows you down, makes you lazy, time is distorted. I know plenty of musicians that did it for a lark or so, but I never knew anybody...well, yes, there have been several real good musicians that were out and out addicts. And therein, I think, lies the danger of the marijuana thing, because I think after awhile it loses its potency. It's like smoking a cigarette. Nothing happens, so you go on to stronger things. Probably the best thing that ever happened to me was that I got busted for it, because God knows, I might have gone into harder things, too, and the guys that did just didn't survive. You can't make it on that scene.

I don't think that any person is greater than their talents and if you don't have your full faculties, your technique is not right. When you play the drums, you try to draw the sound out. When you're on drugs you pound.

God gave you a native talent and a natural feeling of elation when all goes well. You can talk to the biggest junkie and he'll tell you there's no euphoria that can take the place of what nature gave you.

PRIMARY SOURCES

1) Krupa interview for PBS' "Soundstage," 1971

2) Krupa lecture before youth group at County Court Building (Mineola, Long Island), circa November, 1969

THE

SECOND BANDS

1944–1951

CHAPTER SIX

REVIEWS OF THE SECOND BANDS, 1944 - 1951

Barry Ulanov
Metronome Magazine,
September, 1944

Gene had less than a half-hour to do his stuff on this bill (at New York's Capitol Theater), between showings of that megalomanical 1944 version of *East Lynne, Since You Went Away*. And his band was new. So you can't judge this show too harshly. You can make one point, though. You can say with some sadness that Gene Krupa's new band is a lot more commercial and a lot less interesting musically than his old one.

There wasn't a first-rate instrumental in this show. The opening *St. Louis Blues*, the closing *Drum Boogie*, the intermediate *Bolero in the Jungle*, were ordinary flag-wavers, the last-named made more commercial but not more interesting by Gene's tympani solo. The G-Noters sounded like just another vocal quartet in *Swinging on a Star* and *The Hawaiian War Chant*. Peggy Mann sang competently. And Gene offered a smart piece of theater in his bongo-drum version of *Amor*. But there were no kicks of the kind the Krupa-Eldridge-O'Day combination of fond memory used to serve.

Gene is using nine strings in this new organization. Why, I can't tell you. In the scores presented here, they're lost. And, unfortunately, the violins, violas and cello don't play too well together, either. Attack and intonation were poor at the show I caught.

The Capitol gave this show superb staging. Lighting, drops, were in excellent taste, simple but dramatic. It's a shame that with such excellent showcasing, Gene had to make any commercial concessions. With the power of his name and the glory of the Capitol's spotlights, Gene could have, should have, relied entirely on good music to keep his audiences attentive and happy.

Leonard Feather
Metronome Magazine
July, 1945

This was the first time I had seen the Krupa Trio on the concert stage (Town Hall, New York, June 9, 1945). I was disappointed to find that Teddy Napoleon had been replaced by Georgie Walters, whose work was almost amateurish compared with that of his predecessor. I wished that Charlie Venturo's (later changed to Ventura) tenor had been given more to do, instead of being tied up so inextricably in complicated routines with Gene's drums. Gene astonished me with his ever fabulous technique, but left the feeling that the numbers were over-arranged with an eye to visual rather than musical value.

George T. Simon
Metronome Magazine
July, 1945

Gene Krupa popped into Frank Dailey's Newark Terrace Room last month with a band that fits him. Not stringy, less pretentious, more jumping and more blatant. It serves as an excellent showcase for one of the greatest drummers of all time.

Technically the band is far advanced over the sprawling outfit Gene showed in the East last year. The complete absence of sloppy strings helps considerably, and so do the tightly-knit brass and rhythm sections. Gene is doing all the drumming again (except during shows) and the difference is electrifying. He has discovered a fine new bassist, Harry Babison, whose rich tone and strong beat help greatly.

So far as jazz soloists go, there still are the magnificient Charlie Venturo, whose tone isn't quite as thrilling as it used to be, possibly because he's trying too hard to be cute, and Tommy Pederson, one of the great all-around trombonists. There's also a trumpeter named (Vince) Hughes who shows exceptionally pretty taste and a trombonist named (Leon) Cox who tries very hard and gets results a good part of the time. Then there's also a very neat painist, George Walters, plus Buddy Stewart doing very nice ballard singing and a vocal quartet quite above par.

Routine of the band also includes the Krupa Trio of Gene, Venturo and Walters, a smart, showy unit, besides the usual mixing up of jump and ballads. The ensemble swing of the band will doubtless be improved when Gene makes the necessary changes in the saxes which at review time did not possess the rhythmic looseness of the rest of the band. Arrangements by Eddie Finckel and others are still top-notch and should sound even top-notchier once the more relaxed replacements have arrived.

Gene Krupa
Metronome Magazine
September, 1945

Conducting? Well, that was all part of the business of having the string section. The strings really needed a conductor, but — this may sound conceited, but honest, I never could find a drummer who could play on ballads the way I like to hear them. Primarily, I just had to be playing all the time to be happy...The older folks liked them (the strings) all right, but all the youngsters in the audience seemed to go for the wilder stuff. Kids would come up to the bandstand and want to know what we were building with all those fiddles. Aside from that, I couldn't get any one arranger to write consistently well for the strings, so some arrangements were good and some were not so good. And on a lot of dates we played the amplification didn't give them a chance. For instance, when we were in the Palladium six months ago, the strings might as well have gone home for all the audience ever got to hear of them. I still think the string thing could be done right if we were sitting down on a long location job with time to work things out and the right writers. You know, I had dreams of Roy Eldridge playing muted with a fine soft string background and things like that. The vocal quartet? That was purely a commercial idea that didn't seem to materialize. Gee, you don't how how wonderful it is having Anita back with the band. The other evening we played out at Camp Kilmer to about 15,000 fellows who had just returned from overseas. They'd been out of touch with our newer stuff and were shouting out for all the old hits, the ones Anita made with us when she was with the band before. It was a great kick.

George T. Simon
Metronome Magazine
November, 1945

Gene Krupa has set out to make himself a definite personality, with or without drums, and, judged upon the audience reception to this stage show (at New York's Capitol Theater), is succeeding quite well. He did a lot of talking, kissed a movie actress, danced with Anita O'Day and played drums, all within the space of an hour. If I'm not being too bold, I'd like to add that he's still far and away at his best when he plays the drums.

The show, intelligently paced, moved quickly, presenting amusing innovations right from the start. Instead of coming on with the usual flag-waving opener, the band swung from these into a soft, subtly swinging arrangement of *Lover,* with much attention paid to dynamics and the beat. Then came Buddy Stewart, continually improving, with *Till the End of Time*, after which Anita, who had to play second- fiddle to a very poor Pamela Britton, did her one solo, *Ooh, Hot Dawg*, with less than the usual O'Day inspiration. Then she duoed with Buddy in *That Feeling in the Moonlight*, whereupon Gene came along and they trioed through a cute dance routine. With the exception of the whole band tom-tomming and the closing *Drum Boogie*, in which Gene carried on some clever if unconvincing dialogue with his shadow, that was all for the full band. Having Dick and Gene Wesson on the same bill helped tremendously.

Gene and pals have produced a band show a good deal smarter than the usual run-of-the-mill stage show and the band, despite numerous changes, played it well. However, the Trio's *Stompin' at the Savoy,* with Venturo greater than ever, still proved to be the musical highlight. Too bad Gene couldn't have concentrated more on the Trio, instead of upon unnecessary band direction and verbiage.

Laughlin
Metronome
Magazine
March, 1946

The band opened the show (at Los Angeles' Orpheum) with Krupa himself on drums featured in a number called *Leave Us Leap,* in the traditional Krupa opener fashion, where Gene hits everything in sight, plays 'em soft, plays 'em hard, and ends up winded.

Things began to happen when the Trio upstaged for a set of three tunes. Charlie Venturo, Teddy Napoleon and Gene played with real jazz feeling in *Dark Eyes*. Krupa's *Wire Brush Stomp* was standard for his faithful, and Venturo tuned his tenor to Napoleon's piano for some unusually effective passages in *Limehouse*.

The thrill came when Carolyn Grey was introduced. In spite of two unusually poorly selected numbers Miss Grey sang with beautiful intonation, in perfect tune. On *Chickery Chick* she sounded as if she weren't kidding. *Boogie Blues* was a dressed-up *Fine and Mellow*.

Krupa did a production on *Blue Rhythm Fantasy* and followed it by introducing his male singer, Buddy Stewart.

Stewart stayed on for four ballads, the last in cooperation with Carolyn Grey. He sings as well as any of the plethora of crooners on the current market, but he seems over-confident.

The show's closer brought on the Krupa shadowy silhouettes and lighted tom-toms for *Drum Boogie*. Gene would do well to learn more about stage production. The show was long and painful and with the exception of the Trio nothing much happened.

George T. Simon
Metronome
Magazine
June, 1946

Gene Krupa, whose drumming did so much to infect the public with swing and its imitations, is now on a sweet band kick. Proof is not only Gene's verbal admission but also the commissions of his very fine band at the 400 Restaurant in New York.

Though the Krupians pour forth some swing now and then, especially via a trio composed of Gene, Charlie Ventura and Teddy Napoleon, they spend most of any given evening playing the very pretty arrangements of George Williams and Gerry Mulligan, arrangements that give the excellently blended saxes, the pretty-toned trombones, the strong, flexible trumpets, and ballad singer Buddy Stewart ample opportunities. The lesser amount of swing they do play is confined to the aforementioned Trio, to some flag-waverish exhibitions that Gene always has to play to prove that he is Gene Krupa, and a few medium-tempoed works that often center about pretty Carolyn Grey and which give a few of the instrumentalists a change to get off their chairs.

Gene has some good jazzmen. There is, of course, Ventura, who has been a great tenorman but who will have to regain some of his wonderful tonal body and eliminate some stylized tricks before he can satisfy my personal tastes. In addition, there is 18-year-old Reds (sic, means Red) Rodney, a trumpeter of the Dizzy school, who has much imagination and beat harnessed to a style that is not a direct imitation of Gillespie's. Already good, he is bound to develop into something great. There are also two very excellent jazz trombonists, Dick Taylor and Ziggy Elmer, a young altoist named Charlie Kennedy who makes much out of few opportunities, and, of course, the very fine Napoleon on piano.

But Krupa doesn't seem too interested in displaying these soloists. He is prouder of his band as a group, and he has a well-rehearsed, rich-sounding unit to be proud of. Credit goes not only to all individuals, but also in great measure to the lead-men in each section.

The saxists have Harry Terrill, an altoist whom I used to roast with unfailing regularity years back when he played for Mitchell Ayres and whom I now toast with even more fervent ferocity. Recently discharged from the service, Terrill has brought back with a much looser, more fluent style. He now phrases with great rhythmic feeling, while still maintaining his strong, sure tone and his all-around mastery of his instrument.

The trumpets have Joe Griscare (sic, means Triscari), an exceptionally dependable lead powerhouse, while the trombones are paced by Warren Covington, a lad with a gorgeous tone, a tremendous range, and an ability to lead a section well in addition to playing standout pretty solos.

On the subject of prettiness, there is, of course, the very much so Carolyn Grey, who sings even better than she did for Woody. And on the subject of singers there is the very good Buddy Stewart, possessor of a robust voice, a flare for musical phrasing and a sincere personality. And on the subject of personality there is, of course, Gene himself, whose poise improves yearly, who is still one of the all-time greats on drums, but who would please me more if he would devote less time to drumming for effects and more time to settling his band into a real groove wherein it can really rock. Now that the Krupa band can satisfy the customers with its very pretty music, Gene can afford to devote almost no time at all to "swing-for-effect" and a great deal of time to "swing-for-swing's sake." He can do it and he should do it.

Barbara Hodgkins
Metronome
Magazine
October, 1946

Gene always seems to draw a Capitol show that has an overlong picture, cutting the band's time down to half or three-quarters of an hour. But even giving him the benefit of the doubt, I can't feel he made the most of this opportunity. Billed along with Carolyn Grey by the theater were Buddy Stewart and the Jazz Trio: Buddy was out ill, and the Trio did exactly nil. Carolyn sang *Boogie Blues* well, looked very well. Show opened with the familiar Krupa version of *Lover*, and the only other numbers were *Valse*

Triste and *Drum Boogie*, which were nearly 100% Krupa —phosphorescent drumsticks, shadow tricks, and all the old stocks in trade that he's been using for years. Usually, that's what theater audiences go for, but I've never heard so many mutterings about "lousy show" and "didn't like it" as here. It would seem about time that "the old order changeth."

Gene Krupa
Metronome
Magazine
September, 1945

...The critics have a tendency to expect me to be too uncommercial. They're more interested in melody instruments than in drums, so they complain if I take too many solos. Now I can play to suit anybody, I believe. If there's a certain critic in the audience and I know the kind of drums he likes to hear, I can play so that he'll get what he expected and wanted, and I can be sure he'll like it. In fact, quite often I've tried to follow the critics' advice by not featuring myself so much, but you know what happens? People come up to the bandstand and say 'What's the matter, you tired or something?' Even on records, you can build up enough excitement and intensity to justify a long drum solo...Sure, I've followed suggestions by critics sometimes. I'm not above listening to criticism. I never forget that if it weren't for the critics I wouldn't even be a commercial figure today.

Burt Korall
International
Musician
September, 1972

The new Krupa band, in addition to the normal brass, reeds, rhythm complement, had ten strings. Though Gene liked his enlarged orchestra, the fans didn't. After returning to New York from Hollywood, and some picture-making with the "Swing with Strings" band (*George White's Scandals* of 1945), he opened at the Astor Roof with the streamlined, modern outfit. It was to become his best and most musical band.

Gene Krupa
The Big Bands
1967

I guess I must have had the ideas that I was a Kostelanetz or something. Do I regret it? Financially, yes. But it was a good experience.

Gene Krupa
down beat
Magazine
March 5, 1959

I loved it (the band with strings), but people somehow associated me with the role of mad drummer and didn't think I knew anything about music. I started to conduct, but they wouldn't have it. They wanted me to drum.

Gene Krupa
International Musician
September, 1972

We enjoyed success with our records, jazz things like "Leave Us Leap" and Mulligan's "Disc Jockey Jump," novelties and ballads. Through the great audience response to ballads, the band got us into experimentation as well. I asked George Williams to listen to some of the more colorful "serious" composers — Mussorgsky, Rimsky-Korsakoff, Ravel and Stravinsky — and suggested he develop some scores of their material.Out of this came "Valse Triste" (Greig), "The Galloping Comedians" (Kabalevsky), "Firebird Suite" (Stravinsky).

Burt Korall
International Musician
September, 1972

All went extremely well until 1949. Then, many of Gene's key men left for studio jobs and other opportunities. The band began to lose ground, musically. In 1951, the drummer decided to call it quits. He couldn't get the men he wanted. Moreover, life on the road had gotten to be a drag.

Notes to
Gene Krupa and his Orchestra: 1949
(circa 1978)

Gene Krupa was one of a mere handful of swing era bandleaders still actively leading a good big band by 1949. Many leaders had given up the ghost the year before, when another year-long, union-enforced recording ban took away another good source of income from musicians, who had already lost most of the large theaters, nightclubs and ballrooms thorughout the country, due to rising costs. Nonetheless, Gene Krupa kept at it and with a fine big band, composed of some of the best younger jazzmen of the post-war years and one sterling veteran, Roy Eldridge. Eldridge gave up his own swinging combo for the second time to join Krupa in February (1949) and would leave again in the fall to start the first national Jazz At the Philharmonic tour...George 'The Fox' Williams was Gene's principal arranger in the late forties...The Krupa band was resident for a lengthy stay at the famed Hollywood Palladium, and recording for Columbia at this time, although a total of only eight tunes were done in 1949. In 1950 he would switch to RCA and by 1951 his big band days would be over.

George T. Simon
**Metronome
Magazine**
March, 1950

Gene Krupa's recent engagement at Bop City found him with not the best band of his career but still with a musically competent, if not too stimulating crew. Playing a book of mixed arrangements, some modern, others more of the Fletcher Henderson school, his 15-piece band sounded both interesting and uninspired. Section for section, the outfit produced a good sax quintet, thanks in part to Lenny Hambro's lead, a fairly good brass section, with the trombones achieving a better blend than the trumpets, but with Ray Triscari's lead outstanding in the latter quartet. The rhythm section boasted a fine bassist in Don Simpson, and swung on the older type of arrangement, although Gene's style unfortunately doesn't fit bop at all. Outstanding among soloists were Buddy Wise on tenor, especially on slower tunes where his pretty tone showed off; trombonist Urbie Green, a young lad with great facility; and Don Fagerquist at times only, his note-splitting interfering too often with his ideas. More consistency for the band in general, especially in its musical conception, would help Krupa tremendously.

GENE KRUPA ON THE SECOND BAND'S ARRANGEMENTS

What's This? composed by Lambert. Arranged by Budd Johnson Recorded 1/22/45

Budd Johnson, the arranger, got together with (vocalists) Dave Lambert and Buddy Stewart on this one. They were always trying new things, and I guess you could say they were pretty far ahead of the day. Buddy's dead, but Dave's still very active, of course. Hey, you can hear the strings on this one...This grew out of the run we had at the Capitol Theater with rehearsal every night after the third show...we felt there was a crying need for something new, and didn't know what, so we asked the public in the title, "What's This?"

Leave Us Leap, composed and arranged by Ed Finckel. Recorded 2/22/45

This is by the second band, the one with the strings. Yeah, they're in there someplace. Why did I add them? I'd just come off the Dorsey band, and he must have had close to two dozen of them, and I guess I must have had an idea I was a Kostelanetz or something. Do I regret it? Financially, yes. But it was a good experience. The soloist? Don Fagerquist on trumpet and Charlie Ventura on tenor — what a lot of authority he's always had! — and Leon Cox on trombone and Teddy Napoleon on piano.

Body and Soul, composed by Heyman-Sour-Green-Eyton. Arranged by Charlie Ventura. Recorded 3/8/45

I'm glad this is included in this album because it was never heard by too many people before. That's because somebody pirated an earlier version that we did in a concert (probably the Town Hall Concert) and it killed the sale of our Columbia release. It came out on a Disc label, I believe it was, and Charlie and I never got a dime for it. There isn't too much I can say about this, except that we did the number on our first Goodman Trio date and this is one of those ballads I've always enjoyed playing.

Dark Eyes, public domain. Arranged by Charlie Ventura. Recorded 3/8/45

We used the Trio to sort of follow the Goodman pattern. It made a good contrast with the big band, too. As a matter of fact, we made this thing as a throw-in on a date when the strings and saxes and brass had gotten into a big hassle about pitch. I finally got so disgusted that I sent the band home, and so the date shouldn't be a total loss, Charlie (Ventura) and Teddy (Napoleon) and I decided to record this. It turned out to be one of our biggest hits. We'd worked out on it over a period of time, on various dates, so we knew ahead of time just about how we were going to play it...We cut this number and it was voted No. 3 by the nation's disk jockeys for the best combo jazz record of the year.

Opus # One. composed and arranged by Sy Oliver. Recorded 8/21/45

Sy Oliver, who wrote this, also did this arrangement for us. As you may remember, he'd written it when he was in Tommy Dorsey's band, only their arrangement came complete with strings. But we'd gotten rid of ours by this time, and we were back again on the Astor Roof when we recorded it. Anita does a real swinging job on the vocal and that's Don Fagerquist on trumpet.

Boogie Blues, composed by Krupa-Biondi. Recorded 8/21/45

Originally this was called "Tympani Boogie" and it was supposed to feature me on the tymps. But Anita expressed a desire to sing it, and so I forsook my tymps. I don't know where she got those lyrics — she dug them up from somewhere — I think it was from Billie Holiday. That muted trombone behind her is Leon Cox again. I like that also. That's Johnny Bothwell. He always did like Johnny Hodges! You *can hear how much the band admired Lionel Hampton by those riffs toward the end.*

Lover, composed by Rogers-Hart. Arranged by Ed Finckel. Recorded 9/26/45

Believe it or not, but we actually recorded this at eight o'clock in the morning while we were playing at the Capitol Theater in New York. Can you imagine trying to blow at that time of day! I remember we did it on the CBS studio where they now do television shows like Ed Sullivan's and Jackie Gleason's. But what a tempo — strictly what we used to call a killer-diller. But isn't that band clean? And that brass is so great! That's Charlie Ventura on tenor, of course, and Donny Fagerquist on that nice muted trumpet, and that wild trombone is Leon Cox — he's beautiful on this, I tell you!

How High the Moon, composed by Hamilton-Lewis. Arranged by Gerry Mulligan. Recorded 5/21/46

Those trumpets sure played in good time, didn't they? The alto is Charlie Kennedy, a nice, fresh-sounding little guy. The trombone must be Dick Taylor and the trumpet is Fagerquist — no, it's Red Rodney...this was Gerry Mulligan's first arrangement for the band. It's more conservative than Gerry's later work, of course; one gets the feeling that Gerry's notes are saying "I mustn't get too far out." But the boys in the band are blowing as though they're thinking. "This cat's got something fresh, let's see if we can dig what he means." The two soloists who came close are Charlie Kennedy on alto and Red Rodney, trumpet. The ensemble is clean and crisp, to say the least.

There Is No Breeze (To Cool the Flame of Love), composed by Dick-Alstone. Arranged by George Williams. Recorded 9/20/47

George Williams arranged this. He sort of brought the band into a new era. He was very chord-conscious, and used to write those real wide voicings for the sections. It made the band sound very rich and big.

Disk Jockey Jump. Composed and arranged by Gerry Mulligan. Recorded 1/22/47

This was another of our more successful sides. Gerry Mulligan wrote it. As I recall him then, he was a kind of temperamental guy who wanted to expound a lot of his ideas. This one was good musically and commercially. Originally, it was called something else — I can't remember what — but we wanted to attract the disk jockeys, and so that title. This also is Kennedy again; the trombone Dick Taylor; the tenor Buddy Wise, and the trumpet is Fagerquist.

Starburst,
Composed and arranged by Ed Finckel.
Recorded 2/5/47

We used this for our theme for a while during that period when the radio networks and ASCAP couldn't get together and all of us had to scrounge around for new theme songs. I had an idea for a melody, and I asked Eddie Finckel, our arranger, to make up just enough music to give us time to get all the way up as the Capitol Theater pit rose. Actually, it was only a few bars but Mannie Sacks, then the head of Columbia Records, caught our act, liked the theme, and said "Record it!" So Eddie embellished it some more, and this is how it came out. Then, just for a gag, we added that little sign-off, the thing we always played to tell dancers the set was over.

Gene's Boogie,
Composed by Ellis-Williams. Arranged by George Williams.
Recorded 2/5/47

This was a follow-up to "Boogie Blues," which we'd recorded a year and a half earlier and which had become enough of a hit to warrant a follow-up. Unfortunately, we couldn't say that about too many of our records. There's a different girl singer here, a very pretty blonde named Carolyn Grey, who married our drummer, Joe Dale, and who now, by the way, is a helluva fine talent booker out in Las Vegas. This thing became quite a commercial hit, too. The singer on the intro is George Williams, who made the arrangement, and the guy playing that brilliant trumpet is Al Porcino, who's now a star in the Hollywood studios — on trumpet that is.

Calling Dr. Gillespie,
Composed and arranged by Ed Finckel. Recorded 12/29/47

This is slightly boppish. Eddie Finckel wrote it. He had auditioned for us with "Lover," which was a natural for me, and he sort of fell right in with the band after that. The good Dr., of course, is Dizzy, whom the guys in the band admired so much. That went for me, too, because, in addition to opening up new things in jazz, he always played with such great time. The trombonist here is Bob Fitzpatrick, who later went with Stan Kenton; the piano is Teddy Napoleon, and that very pretty tenor is Buddy Wise.

I Should Have Kept on Dreaming, Composed by George Williams and Gene Krupa. Arranged by George Williams. Recorded 12/29/47

Say, I never heard this before! That's right, it was never issued...I used to love to play this thing. Gee, that's so pretty, the way Charlie (Kennedy) plays. And that arrangement is so good. George Williams wrote it...I'm so glad this thing is in there. I think it gives you a good idea of how musical the band was and how well it could do things other than the usual jump numbers everybody expected from us.

Up an Atom, Composed and arranged by Ed Finckel. Recorded 12/29/47

You know, when I hear sides as good as this, it sort of bolsters my ego. I didn't realize that we'd made so many good records. That's (Don) Fagerquist again, and Buddy Wise and Bob Fitzpatrick.

Bop Boogie, Composed and arranged by George Williams. Recorded 1/26/49

This one's arranged by George (The Fox) Williams, and sung by Dolores Hawkins, who is now doing great on her own. Quite a few bands rode into prominence with numbers arranged in this vein. "Bop Boogie" was conceived as a production number for a movie short. Roy Eldridge's screaming trumpet is most exciting, and the band has a good modern sound. I'd say it was definitely one of Dolores' stepping stones toward doing a single.

Lemon Drop, Composed by George Wallington. Recorded 1/26/49

Now we're coming into an even more modern era of the band. (Bassist) Chubby Jackson had recorded this first, and I always loved it. It's George Wallington's composition, and you can tell how much the guys enjoyed playing it just by the enthusiasm on this record. The bongos helped out a lot on this one, but of course the big hero of the side is Frankie Rosolino, who sang and played trombone. We made a movie short of this thing, too.

AFTERTHOUGHTS BY GENE

You know, I feel awfully good about these things...I was always rather proud of the records we made, but I never realized how many good ones there were. But now, as I begin to look back at the band from the very beginning, it occurs to me that there are even some other things that aren't in this collection that I'd like to hear again. That's what time does — it makes you forget all sorts of things, good as well as bad; and then, when something like this comes along to stir up memories, suddenly you begin to remember so many things, and the past becomes alive again, and it makes being alive today seem even more worthwhile...Lest you think I dwell only in the past, let me say that I hope to make many more sides and that some real good ones will be forthcoming, some that in the future will also warrant a place in the history of jazz.

THE

BLINDFOLD

TEST

CHAPTER SEVEN

GENE KRUPA BLINDFOLD TEST

Leonard Feather
Metronome Magazine November, 1950

Gene Krupa was given no information whatever about the records played for him either before or during his "Blindfold Test."

(1) **Ray Bauduc,** *When My Sugar Walks Down The Street* **(Capitol).**Nate Kazebier, trumpet; Matty Matlock, clarinet; Brad Gowans, trombone; Stan Wrightsman, piano; Ray Bauduc, drums.

Krupa:*I guess this was made with the intention of fitting into that Dixieland idea that's commercial right now. At first I thought it was Schroeder on piano, but no, it's not that bunch of guys. LaRocca on cornet? Matlock on clarinet? I haven't heard him in a long time. Trombone's tone sounds like Cutty Cutshall, but it's not as rhythmic as he usually plays. Solos didn't kill me, and the rhythm just pounded. No subtleties. The drummer? No idea. Two stars.*

(2) **Benny Goodman Sextet,** *Blue Lou* **(Capitol).** Goodman, clarinet; Doug Mettome, trumpet; Wardell Gray, tenor; Buddy Greco, piano; Sonny Igoe, drums.

Krupa: *First off, that's got to be Buddy DeFranco — awful good clarinet. Trumpet's very clean; may be Navarro or McGhee. I don't recognize the tenor, but I like that slightly Hawkins sound. The group has a nice ensemble tone, yet it gets a jam quality and feeling. Drummer fits right into what they're doing, too. Nice piano. I'd call this an excellent record to play for someone who doesn't like bop — to change his mind. Three stars.*

(3) **Sy Oliver,** *Wagon Wheels* **(Decca).** Arranger, Sy Oliver.

Krupa*: That's got to be Duke. I can recognize it by Johnny Hodges and Carney and the rest of them. With all this drive to make Americans dance music conscious, that's the kind of music they should become dance-conscious to. Melodic, with good full brass, and it's something anyone can dig. It's colorful, too. A hell of a record. Give it three and a half.*

(4) **Dave Barbour,** *Harlem Mambo* **(Capitol).**

Krupa*: These horns sound too Americanized to be what's-his-name, the original guy that made the mambo — Prado? This might be an authentic Cuban rhythm section, but all around, for this vein, I'd almost prefer something with less musicianship and more real feeling. The horns just don't get the authentic beat. I've heard small groups in little dives that really show you what a wonderful, vital part of music Afro-Cuban and similar kinds of music can be. This is just fair. Two stars.*

(5) **Charlie Parker,** *Klaunstance* **(Savoy).** Parker, alto; Miles Davis, trumpet; Max Roach, drums.

Krupa*: Of course it's Charlie's group. I've heard Charlie play lot better — this seems to be more of a show of technique. Trumpet didn't move me too much. You've got to give Max credit for keeping up that tempo. In fact, I like the drumming better than anything else on the record. Max is awful good. By the way, I thought the "Parker with Strings" album was great; he played so pretty with that background. Give this two and a half.*

(6) **Count Basie,** *Bluebeard Blues* **(Columbia).** Arranger, Neal Hefti; Basie, piano; Buddy DeFranco, clarinet; Buddy Rich, drums; Jimmy Lewis, bass.

Krupa*: Tasty drummer — clean as a whistle, whoever he is. Could that be Max? Clarinet is definitely Buddy DeFranco. This sounds like a Basie group and a Neal Hefti arrangement. Basie music with a bop flavor. It has nice time, doesn't scuffle at all. Bass is excellent, too. Three and a half.*

(7) **Reinhold Svensson Quintet,** *Sweet and Lovely* **(New Jazz).** Svensson, piano; Ulf Line, vibes.

Krupa*: The last Shearings I heard were the ones he made in England, I believe. There seems to be a hell of a difference here; vibes has more attack than the gal (Marjorie*

Hyams). But I hear some piano things that you'd have to call Shearing. But then, the guitar doesn't sound like Chuck (Wayne). I guess it's not the Shearing group after all. Is it a West Coast group? This lacks the Shearing subtleties and musicianship. Two stars.

(8) Woody Herman, *Music to Dance To* **(Capitol).** Composer and arranger, Al Cohn; Woody Herman, clarinet; Bill Harris, trombone; Bob Graf, tenor.

Krupa: *This sounds like a white band — pretty stiff. The guys sound like they're finding the arrangement pretty difficult to play, and they had to work like hell to play it anywhere near clean — and after they got through it, it was still nothing much. I don't know the soloists. If this arranger were writing for me I'd give the number right back to him. Maybe it needed a couple more soloists to make it come off. One star.*

(9) Eddie Condon, *Sweet Cider Time, When You Were Mine* **(Decca).** Wild Bill Davison, trumpet; Cutty Cutshall, trombone; Peanuts Hucko, clarinet; Jimmy Atkins, vocal.

Krupa: *It's Condon's group with Cutshall, Peanuts and Wild Bill. That's a feather in their cap, that they get a sound you can recognize right off. They must have had a bad time with that vocalist. It would be better, commercially and musically, to stick to instrumentals, because these guys can play. Give the men an A for effort, but give it two stars.*

Krupa's afterthoughts: *Sure, I can name some four-star records. The original version of Basie's "One O'Clock Jump," the one with Herschel and Lester (Young); Dizzy's "Manteca;" Duke's "Cotton Tail" and — oh, gangs of Ellingtons. My own best? Musically and commercially, I'd say "Rockin Chair."*

I'm glad you like our Fats Waller album, but did you know "Bonaparte's Retreat" has sold better than 200,000? To stay in business nowadays you have to play everything — rhumbas, waltzes, and that hillbilly-type Dixie. And I'm happy to say we're still in business.

END OF AN ERA

AND THE BEGINNING

OF THE JAZZ TRIO

CHAPTER EIGHT

END OF AN ERA AND THE BEGINNING OF THE JAZZ TRIO

In 1946, the big band boom began its steady decline, what with the continuation of the government-imposed 20% amusement tax, high prices bands demanded due to exorbitant salaries draft-free musicians received, the rise in popularity of vocal performers as single attractions, the demise of the American public's "celebratory feeling" which immediately followed the war, subsequent closing of ballrooms, increasing "films only" policy of theater-owners, the development of be-bop and ultimate popularity of small group jazz. Though some bands developed and flourished in the 1946-50 period, including, for a time, Stan Kenton's, Woody Herman's and Dizzy Gillespie's, by the end of 1946 Goodman, Herman, Tommy Dorsey, Harry James, Les Brown and other lesser bands disbanded (James, Herman and Dorsey later reformed).

1946-1947 were relatively good years for the Krupa organization. The fiddle section had been dropped, the band was swinging and the new music of arrangers like Gerry Mulligan and instrumentalists like Red Rodney brought a certain freshness, and even a hit in the form of *Disc Jockey Jump*. Krupa, too, jumped on the be-bop bandwagon: The band, at one time during this period was outfitted in bopster berets, floppy ties and horn-rimmed glasses.

But by 1950, the big band business was at its lowest ebb: Count Basie had been forced to reduce to a septet, Woody Herman broke up his "Four Brothers" aggregation to take a small group to Cuba, Benny Goodman toured Europe with a six-piece outfit, and even the mighty Duke Ellington crew was at its worst economic and possibly musical point in its long history.

Gene Krupa remained a major entertainment name — albeit not a major musical influence — by 1950, but economics and public tastes were closing in on him, the band sounded tired and sluggish, as did Krupa's drumming. A "road scandal" of sorts — three of Gene's young crew were busted for drugs in Detroit in 1950 causing eviction from a hotel and cancellation of an engagement at the Eastwood Gardens — didn't help. Krupa even tried a Dixie group within the band, some out-and-out commercial Dixie recordings with hillbilly vocalist Bobby Soots (and surprisingly, one Soots recording, *Bonaparte's Retreat,* made it to the Top Twenty in 1950), and finally, a switch to the RCA label, which yielded some downright boring, though danceable sides, in the form of a set entitled *Gene Krupa Plays Fats Waller*. Krupa finally decided to break up the big band at the end of 1950, but came back in February of 1951 with a cut-down version of 12 men and two singers. That didn't last till the end of the year.

Why didn't Krupa give up the big band ghost sooner? Though he had surely tired of the road, the one-nighters and responsibilities, it is probably accurate to conclude that, despite his enormous success with the Gene Krupa Jazz Trio as an "added attraction" within the band, he simply felt stylistically insecure away from the big band format. Certainly, Krupa had been identified with the big band since 1935. Would the public accept him under different circumstances? Styles had undergone drastic changes and Krupa tried to accommodate, but he was never a modern percussionist in the sense that Max Roach and Kenny Clarke were, and he likely faced the prospect of "standing out" in a small group with trepidation. As Marty Napoleon says in Chapter Sixteen, he couldn't make it in a be-bop small band, and the big band days were clearly over. And what of the prospect of being a sideman, featured or otherwise? That's difficult when one has been a leader for 13 years both economically and psychologically. And Gene Krupa remained an international star in 1951 and was still known — at least in the eyes of the general public if not the hard-core jazz purists and devotees — as "the world's greatest drummer."

The problem was in finding the right format, one that would properly spotlight Gene Krupa and one that would, musically, transcend styles. Touring with the Jazz At The Philharmonic troupe provided an immediate answer. Charlie Ventura said that it was his suggestion to reform the original Gene Krupa Jazz Trio with Teddy Napoleon in January of 1952. It sounded good on paper: Ventura, as leader of his own enormously successful "Bop for the People" groups, had taken on some of the stylistic devices of be-bop, which would satisfy the "modern jazz" fans, and had become reasonably fluent on the alto, soprano, baritone and bass saxophones in addition to his tenor. CV's four horns would compensate for the lack of tonal variation. Teddy Napoleon would provide the anchor, making up for, as he always did, the absence of a bass. It was The Gene Krupa Jazz Trio that ultimately provided the solution, and helped Krupa make the transition to small groups. And it was a format he successfully presented, in one form or another, for over 20 years.

MUSICAL CONCESSIONS AND BAND TROUBLE/1948

Gene Krupa
Metronome Magazine,
September, 1948

I'm sick and tired of being classed as just a noise-maker. I like to think of myself as a creator of sounds! Our style? It's a mixture. In addition to some modified bop, we play ballads and also some arrangements of the classics which George Williams has been writing for us. They're different from the usual adaptations that you hear. We don't do it like Freddy Martin does or like Glenn Miller did. We want to give the listener an idea of what a whole composition sounds like, and so instead of just taking one theme we take all the important ones. We break up tempos and make it more or less of a concert affair. You'd be surprised how our audiences go for it. Down in Alabama one night the thing that broke up the dance completely was our concert adaptation of Stravinsky's "Firebird Suite"...And we're bringing good music to the dancing public instead of those stinking ballads that the music publishers are forcing down their throats.

Progressive jazz? That progressive jazz is progressive, but it's not jazz...I have to (adapt stylistically to be-bop drumming), because my soloists, like Charlie Kennedy, are so young that they don't know anything but bop. I'm older and have had more experience, so I figure it's easier for me to go their way than for them to go mine. We all like jazz, so why not pull together instead of one faction always trying to tear down the other one. I like bop and I like Dixie...It's all in performance, and if a guy or a band plays one musical style well, then let's encourage him. Let's discourage bad musicianship, and I mean by that the mickey-mouse bands. By merely fighting among ourselves, we're giving those no-goods just that much more of a chance to get ahead of us.

We've got to preserve our rights. When business starts getting really bad, as the offices will have you believe it's starting to get, that's when the promoters start dictating to you. Unfortunately most people don't have too much respect for musicians as human beings. We've become dogs just because of the behavior of a few...

Bookers? Take my band, for example. Only two guys in the entire MCA organization have even bothered to come out and really hear us, Joe Kayser in Chicago and Frank Nichols in New York. Sure, the rest may come to an opening and talk all through everything we do, but if they're going to make a living off us, they should know what we're really like. Do you know that out in the Midwest recently one of the MCA guys tried to sell us as a sweet band on the strength of our record "Lover?" Obviously he hadn't even bothered to listen to the record before he sent it on to the promoter. That sort of thing is typical...

(George T. Simon comments: "He feels that he hasn't received his due, financially speaking, for all he has done. Not only do the booking offices come in for their share of Krupa criticism, but ditto the personal managers. Gene feels very strongly that he has been taken to the cleaners, that he has been badly advised, that the wool has been pulled too far over his eyes by personal managers who tell him 'Everything is all right; you just take care of the music end, Gene, old boy, and we'll take care of the business end.' They took care of it all right, feels Gene, but not for Krupa.")

It's the same way in all entertainment. Take a look at all the top stars who have wound up with nothing...It all comes back to that old, corny cliche: If you want something done, do it yourself.

END OF THE BIG BAND/1950-1951

Gene Krupa
down beat
Magazine,
August 25, 1950

Things look good. In certain parts of the country, things are mighty rough, but the overall picture is a vast improvement over the same scene of a year ago. Business has been great, and I'm not saying that by way of a boast. If it's good with us it must be good with a lot of the other name bands. Last year it was good for mighty few.

We made most of our tour long before the present conflict started, and Korea meant little more than a spot in a geography book. Maybe there'll be a war boom like there was last time in our business, but I think things are improving even without fast-spending defense workers and servicemen anxious to spend their few bucks on a short leave.

I'm pretty enthusiastic about the current band situation. Public tastes have changed drastically since the end of World War II and they're still changing. I think the ultimate result will be a return of good music — the real good type we knew as swing — by public acclaim. You can't stuff anything they don't want down the throats of the people, especially those who patronize ballrooms. That was proven by the story of bop.

I think there's a definite place for bop in the jazz picture, but the timing was bad when it was handed out to the people. They didn't dig it and didn't want to bother to learn what it was all about. They were more interested in dancing. I guess we're all a little guilty of trying to force bop on them. We played our share of it in this band, but it received good reception only in scattered spots — a few college kids were with it and some of the jazz disciples around New York, Chicago and Hollywood caught on. But on the whole, it was a lost cause. As a result, the kids turned to anything and, at that time, the first item was a thing called "Four Leaf Clover." We even had to put it in our books, but we did it with tongue in cheek. We liked to think we were doing it for laughs, even if some of the customers took it seriously.

We're all familiar with the surge of old-time tunes that have made their comeback during the last one and one-half years, many with the benefit of community singing arrangements. That's what they were playing when I was a kid in school. And that's when I first turned to Dixieland out in Chicago. Jazz made quite a march into popularity back in those twenties, and the same thing has happened again.

Even while the "Clovers" and "Cruising Down the Rivers" were sweeping the country, we used to get requests from many patrons for some old Dixieland items. But, stubborn-like, we were confining our jazz items to the bop school. We learned, and last fall, put our first Dixieland number in the books. Like our treatment of "Four Leaf Clover," we did this, too, in a kidding way, probably afraid somebody might take us seriously and laugh at our "backward" ideas. But when we played "Twelfth Street Rag," particularly at college dances, everybody swarmed onto the floor, not to watch our antics but to dance, many doing the Charleston. It was an amazing revelation. So that's when we decided to give them what they want.

We concentrated on plain, full band arrrangements of standard tunes and pop ballads in good sensible dance tempo. For our jazz department we formed a small combo from within the band and dug up the old tunes on which I was brought up with Eddie Condon and his gang out in Chicago so many years ago. To give it a bit different touch, we added a novelty hillbilly singer whom I found in Chicago, Bobby Soots. The result? Those Dixieland items, like "Bonaparte's Retreat" and "At the Jazz Band Ball" have been murdering the customers every place we play. They love it!

I think history will repeat itself. Just as Dixie paved the way for swing and public appreciation of real good music, I think the current trend will lead to the same goal, only in less time. I think that within a year we'll find a demand for bands built along the lines of the old Benny Goodman, Tommy and Jimmy Dorsey, Barnet, Lunceford, Chick Webb, Ellington, and other outfits of that era of the thirties. Listen to the records those bands made 10 to 15 years ago. They're still great. And the people who patronized those outfits know their music and their musicians. They recognized talent as quickly as a leader did and they seldom picked a dud.

What happened to all that? Everyone has an opinion and they add up to a varied lot. Regardless of the cause, some changes happened, much to the dismay of all of us who like to play good music for an appreciative audience. But if the indications we observed in the last few months, from the Carolinas to Texas to San Diego, from Seattle to Salt Lake City to Chicago and New England, mean what they did two decades ago, we're on our way back to some real good music.

There will always be novelty stuff, of course, just as we had "Music Goes 'Round" and "Bei Mir Bist due Schon" and such items in the swing era, but the big rage will be good, solid dance music and a general public appreciation of good jazz, swing, or whatever you want to call it.

1951

Broadcast over Mason City, Iowa's KRIB Radio, August 1950, printed in **down beat Magazine,** June 18, 1952

I don't think we're accomplishing as much today as in the "Leave Us Leap" days. Creatively, no. We've stuck our necks out too many times and we've been hurt by it too many times. You pioneer something and people don't actually know what you're doing. If you make a "name" that way, for instance, Kenton's made his name that way, and the wilder he gets, I guess, the better people like it. I don't know.

Why do middle-aged people like to revert back to older things? Nostalgia, I'd say. If I went out to hear Jimmie Noone—many years from now, up in heaven—I'd immediately ask him to play "I Know That You Know" because that's what I associate Noone with. If I got with Art Tatum I'd want to hear him play "Sweet Lorraine" for some reason or other. I don't know why.

You mustn't put progress itself down, because we'd stay in the same place. But, when it is put before the public, it's got to be presented in a sensible manner, or else we're going to retrogress. In other words, the reason for all that corn that came forth for a while was because people just got a little bit too tired of trying to listen too hard.

After all, music is meant to be enjoyed. I've heard about the sayings of great composers, guys like Bach, and the modernists, say Rimsky-Korsakoff, Ravel, Debussy and particularly Delius. They said that the fact that musicians enjoyed their music so much didn't kill them so much, because they enjoyed what it represented on paper; whereas, when the average public enjoyed it, they enjoyed it for the sheer beauty of it. They reached these people through a medium of art, rather than a medium of mathematics.

Younger kids are more exuberant in their playing...and you can teach them the way you want'em. An older guy, even though he has every good intention in the world, still may have faults. But bop is even old now, you know. If I had to go back? I think the guy that I can feed the best — hat's a term for what a drummer does to a soloist that plays in front of him — I guess the old man is about the best, Benny Goodman; Harry James, Ziggy Elman, Roy Eldridge, a very special favorite of mine, he plays very good. Jess Stacy is good, Teddy Wilson, Lionel Hampton, all those cats.

Those guys were notable not only in the style they played. If those guys were boppin' today they'd be equally as great because personalities in music like they have can't be denied. It'll come forward regardless of what style they're playing. It takes a little while (for a young musician to develop such a personality). They're playing in this new, confused vein, and you've got to learn to walk before you can run, you know. A kid you will hear from — he's bound to make a splash for himself if he does it the right way — is Stan Getz. He's strictly a bopper, but he gets something a little more than the usual.

FEBRUARY, 1952/KRUPA REORGANIZES TRIO AND TRAVELS TO JAPAN APRIL 19TH

---

down beat Magazine, June 18, 1952

It was the most tremendous thing I've ever experienced, even greater than any of the big days with Goodman. Man, we saw nothing but cameras. Every time you turned around a dozen bulbs would go off. I'd like to go back, but the bookings would have to be better. It was great but awfully rough.

OCTOBER, 1954/THE TRIO TRAVELS TO AUSTRALIA

**down beat
Magazine,**
November 3, 1954

Greatest country I've been in on any of my overseas travels. Wonderful people, and all of them seem to be crazy about American jazz. They like all kinds. They don't break up into cliques or schools as they seem to do in the States. The same people who are fanatics about Armstrong are just as enthusiastic about Brubeck or Gerry Mulligan. Just because a fan collects records of the swing bands like Benny doesn't mean he hasn't an equal interest in Kenton. It seemed to me they bought out any good jazz records of all types, as many as the dealers could stock.

Of course, the market isn't flooded with the platters of any individual artist or certain style, which may be the reason they aren't so biased in their preferences.

Honestly, they were the most enthusiastic audience I've played for. I think they even topped the receptions we used to get here in the States in the old days when swing was the rage. In every city we played they greeted us with street parade receptions, ticker-tape style with each of the three of us (Krupa, Eddie Shu, Teddy Napoleon) in a private touring car. We were front page copy in the press and, on our professional appearances, usually played in boxing rings. Sports arenas were the only places that could accommodate the crowds — 70,000 they told us, for 11 concerts.

Bop? They dig it, they play it, but give an equally fair shake to swing, waltzes, regular fox trots, and other such more commercial but danceable styles.

Mel Tormé described this shot, taken while with Goodman circa 1937, as "a killer."
AUTHOR'S COLLECTION.

Gene (third from left), age 13 with brother Pete (to Gene's left) in Chicago. FRANK DRIGGS COLLECTION.

Goodman days, July, 1936, for filming of "The Big Broadcast of 1937." DUNCAN P. SCHIEDT.

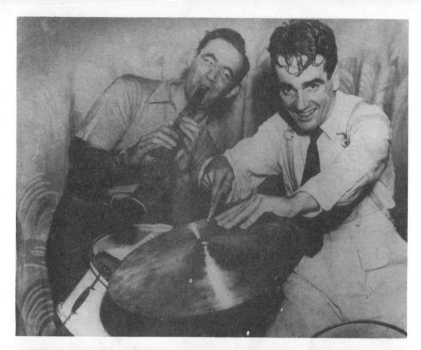

Gene and Benny, circa 1935.
DUNCAN P. SCHIEDT.

Shortly after leaving BG, 1938.
SLINGERLAND DRUM COMPANY.

Gene Krupa

BG Trio being filmed for
"Hollywood Hotel," 1937.
DUNCAN P. SCHIEDT.

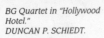

First band, 1938. Note
"Hollywood Hotel" inset.
SLINGERLAND DRUM
COMPANY.

BG Quartet in "Hollywood
Hotel."
DUNCAN P. SCHIEDT.

Publicity shot from feature
film, "Some Like it Hot,"
1938. Gene was billed
as an actor under Bob
Hope and Shirley Ross. Sam
Musiker (clarinet), Ray
Biondi (guitar), Bruce
Squires (trombone), Musky
Ruffo (alto sax), possibly
Sam Donahue (tenor sax).

With ex-cohorts BG and
Harry James, 1940.
DUNCAN P. SCHIEDT.

With Barbara Stanwyck during filming of
"Ball of Fire," 1941.
DUNCAN P. SCHIEDT.

Gene Krupa

Stumping for War Bonds, 1944.
STEVE BROCKWAY.

En route to Hollywood via
Army B-17, 1944.
DUNCAN P. SCHIEDT.

The Jazz Trio with Charlie
Ventura and Teddy
Napoleon, 1945.
DUNCAN P. SCHIEDT.

Film star, now celebrity endorser for Bromo, 1940.
FRANK DRIGGS.

Tommy Dorsey sits in at Hollywood Palladium, 1943.
FRANK DRIGGS.

The Band That (really didn't) Swing With Strings, 1944.
FRANK DRIGGS.

Gene Krupa

With Saul Goodman of the
New York Philharmonic in
Gene's Yonkers basement,
circa 1951.
*MODERN DRUMMER
MAGAZINE.*

Closeup, in solo, from "Beat
the Band."
DUNCAN P. SCHIEDT.

JATP days, 1953, with
Benny Carter as The Trio's
reed.
STEVE BROCKWAY.

The Jazz Trio in Tokyo,
1952, Ventura on bass sax.
FRANK DRIGGS.

Sans strings in 1947's "Beat
the Band." Marty Napoleon
on piano, Red Rodney (to
Gene's left) on trumpet,
Gerry Mulligan)to Gene's
right) on alto sax. Note
"tenor man" Jackie Cooper
on far right.
DUNCAN P. SCHIEDT.

95

Gene Krupa

On the road with The Quartet, mid-1950s, with Eddie Shu (tenor sax), Bobby Scott (piano), John Drew (bass).
MODERN DRUMMER MAGAZINE.

With Roy Eldridge backstage at JATP, mid-1950s.
CHUCK STEWART.

With Garry Moore on CBS Television, mid-1950s.
FRANK DRIGGS.

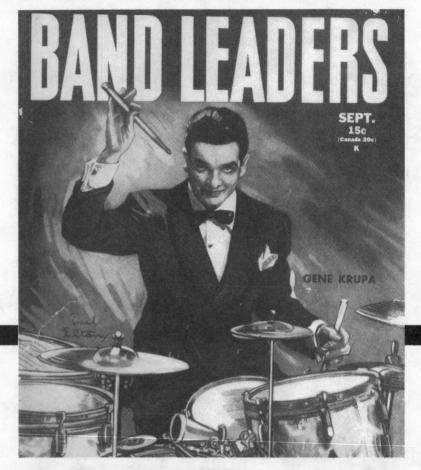

Cartoonish rendering, nevertheless gracing the cover of "Band Leaders" fanzine, July, 1945. AUTHOR'S COLLECTION.

Celebrating the opening of the Krupa-Cole Drum School, 1954, with Cozy Cole (right) and Barney Bigard. AUTHOR'S COLLECTION.

*"Chicago and All That Jazz"
television special,
late-1950s, with Eddie
Condon (guitar), Wild Bill
Davison (cornet), Jack
Teagarden (trombone), Bud
Freeman (tenor sax), Pee
Wee Russell (clarinet),
probably Mort Herbert
(bass).
CHUCK STEWART.*

*One of the "Timex"
television specials,
late-1950s, with (left to
right) Steve Allen, Woody
Herman and Teagarden in
background.
AUTHOR'S COLLECTION.*

"The Gene Krupa Story,"
with Susan Kohner as
wife-to-be Ethel and Sal
Mineo as Gene, 1959.
*ACADEMY OF MOTION
PICTURE ARTS AND
SCIENCES.*

In Frankfurt, West
Germany jazz fest, playing
on Dave Bailey's drums,
mid-1950s.
MICHAEL MONTFORT.

100

Photographer Chuck
Stewart's classic study
of Gene, circa 1962.

Great New Quartet, a few
months later, locale
unknown.
MODERN DRUMMER
MAGAZINE.

1960 CBS television spot
with Mel Tormé, Neal Hefti
(trumpet), others unknown.
FRANK DRIGGS.

The Great New Quartet,
with Ventura, John Bunch
(piano), "Knobby" Totah
(bass) at The Embers in
Indianapolis, February,
1964.
DUNCAN P. SCHIEDT.

With Buddy Rich in the
studio, presumably
preparing to record one of
the drum duels for the
"Burnin' Beat" album in
January, 1962. Despite
photo, contractor Eddie
Wasserman claims the two
never actually recorded
"together" on the album.
CHUCK STEWART.

102

GENE KRUPA

The final Zildjian publicity photo, about 1970. AVEDIS ZILDJIAN COMPANY.

On Buddy Rich's drums at Rich's nightclub during party for Gene, circa 1971. ADVEDIS ZILDJIAN COMPANY.

1971 Krupa and Rich battle for Canadian television, with Lionel Hampton, Gerry Mulligan (in white jacket), Milt Hinton (bass), Mel Lewis (drums in rear). SLINGERLAND DRUM COMPANY.

October, 1972, PBS television reunion of the BG Quartet. DUNCAN P. SCHIEDT.

With long-time friend Armand Zildjian at the same gathering. AVEDIS ZILDJIAN COMPANY.

The final Krupa-Ventura reunion, in Philadelphia in December, 1971.
AUTHOR'S COLLECTION.

Urban League Tribute to Lionel Hampton, New York's Waldorf-Astoria in February, 1973.
STEVE BROCKWAY.

*The man who sold a million
sets of drums and inspired
millions of drummers,
about 1935.
MODERN DRUMMER
MAGAZINE.*

THE

SMALL GROUPS

1952–1970

CHAPTER NINE

REVIEWS OF THE SMALL GROUPS, 1952-1970

Norman Granz,
notes to **Norman
Granz' Jazz At The
Philharmonic
featuring The Gene
Krupa Trio**
 June, 1952.

Krupa decided to form a trio within his orchestra, and selected Charlie Ventura on tenor saxophone and Teddy Napoleon on piano for it. The Trio literally worked out arrangements among themselves, and achieved a sound that far surpassed that which three people have heretofore usually managed to attain. Krupa used the Trio as a kind of specialty whenever his orchestra played...I was very fortunate in being able to present the Gene Krupa Trio in its first concerts, along with Jazz At The Philharmonic's regular group of musicians...Musicians like Krupa, Ventura and Napoleon generally play to the audience, and this time the audience responded so effusively that the Trio played better than it had ever played before.

Gagh
Variety
February 20, 1952

The Gene Krupa Trio, which includes the drummer leader, Charlie Ventura on tenor sax and Teddy Napoleon at piano, has been a jazz favorite for years. Krupa used to spotlight the Trio with his large orchestra and it later was a presentation on the Norman Granz "Jazz At The Philharmonic" concerts. Ventura, who now owns the Open House Club on the White Horse Pike, in South Jersey, got Krupa and Napoleon together again to join him in workouts as an act at the club. Combo is solid and satisfying for the jazz crowd, and showy enough musically to hold more general interest. Three men literally knock themselves out each set working for 45 minutes to an hour without a letup. Of interest is the resetting of Krupa's *Drum Boogie* (long the piece de resistance of his band concerts) for three instruments. Spot from floor plays on drummer to heighten showiness. It is hardly a secret that Krupa is one of the greatest of the skins and can put out an infinite variety of stuff. In *Perdido*, for example, he takes a four-minute break and never once loses them. Ventura's pre-eminence on the tenor sax is also well established, and he does well by the baritone and alto horns, which he employs for a change of sound. Ventura cannot only drive with the best for the tenors, but he also modulates the instrument for expression and has such added assets as invention and humor. Teddy Napoleon is a tricky executant of the keyboard, and his smiling, relaxed style at the piano doesn't lessen to any degree his skill and proficiency. The Trio uses all head arrangements and their offerings are principally standards: *Body and Soul, Stomping at the Savoy, Sweet Lorraine, Dark Eyes, Flyin' Home*, etc. Numbers all run long, the shortest about six or seven minutes, but these can be tightened in future workouts for more concise state or TV timing.

Pit
Variety
December 24, 1958

Gene Krupa is a safe bet to keep a nice head of b.o. steam up over the holidays (at Chicago's London House). He doubtless rates as one of the strongest personalities in the pop and jazz fields, and his skinbeating is still inimitable. He can range from down-to-business stickwork to the showmanly ways that have long identified him, when he put the sticks to the bass strings on *Big Noise From Winnetka*. The combo's library and readings plead no single cause and there's enough in each set to please the ordinary enthusiast (as in *Heart of My Heart* with its strong melody line) or the snob set, per a delicate, flute-featured treatment of *September Song*, a subtle item with Far East overtones via Krupa's cymbals. There's the usual wild outpouring for the unit's *Drum Boogie*, which has long bore the Krupa patent. The sidemen (probably Eddie Wasserman, reeds; Ronnie Ball, piano; Jimmy Gannon, bass) are plenty spotlighted, but the hoopla's for Krupa, and that's the way the cash register rings.

Stephen Frostberg
notes to *Big Noise
From Winnetka*:
**Gene Krupa at the
London House** 1959

As an ensemble, and in terms of good taste and inventiveness, this is the best "working" combo Gene has played with since his old Goodman Trio and Quartet days. The modern concept of the drummer in the ensemble as a sometimes melodic voice has not escaped Gene. His role now is much broader than it was in the Goodman chamber groups. He gives himself plenty of solo space, true, but he also emerges as an active conversationalist with the other instruments. He riffs and provides melodious "fills" when somebody else is soloing. His deft, crisp brush work still is in a class by itself, even in this new age of virtuoso drummers. To these ears (Eddie) Wasserman is a decided improvement over earlier Krupa tenor men. In the Lester Young-Stan Getz lineage, he plays with lyricism and sensitivity — no tasteless exhibitionism here, no whining sound.

Jose
Variety
March 8, 1961

On a quick interim bill, Basin Street East has a highly diverted set of entertainers. The event is distinguished by the return of Gene Krupa to his labors after a lengthy hospital siege, for the second run of Pat Harrington, Jr. in New York and the chirping of Anita O'Day. From the days of his indenture to Benny Goodman to his present eminence, Krupa has been a skilled skin specialist. In the beginning he used a powerful physique, but this style has been gradually changed to a mature viewpoint. There are parts of his beating in which he doesn't spare himself. There are also moments of controlled rowdiness and flashy showmanship. But for the main part his beats are strong and assertive without being blatant. His major moment comes when his colleagues on the bandstand desert same to give Krupa an exclusive on the spotlight for a lengthy and showmanly session. His fellow musicians, headed by Eddie Wasserman on sax, give him staunch support.

Dom Cerulli notes
to **The Great New
Gene Krupa Quartet featuring Charlie Ventura,**January
- February, 1964

Teamed with Gene in his 1964 version of the Gene Krupa Quartet, a group that seems to grow younger with each passing year, is sax man Charlie Ventura...The magic of the Krupa name and sound are still with us. But if the listener will listen closely, he'll find that Gene Krupa not only means drums, but also means beguiling small group jazz...This is 1964, and the group crackles with energy.

Bernie Brown
down beat
Magazine
December 2, 1965

His quartet, Eddie DeHaas, bass; Carmen Leggio, tenor saxophone; and Dick Wellstood, piano, has plenty of bookings. They do about 20 to 25 weeks in the New York area, about four weeks a year at the London House, and then play Baker's in Detroit, and Al Hirt's in New Orleans. *Actually, we've got more jobs than we can handle,* Krupa said.

Luiz
Variety
May 10, 1967

Gene Krupa, backed by a combo of bass, sax and piano (probably Eddie Shu, reeds; Dick Wellstood, piano; Benny Moten, bass), generates plenty of enthusiasm at Al Hirts' French Quarter bistro (New Orleans) where he opened a two-week stand Monday. Krupa, playing a return, is a perfectionist who knows exactly what his audience is looking for. He displays a mastery of the drums in an hour long show. He displays a mastery of the first, then a staccato frenzy with many improvisations to win hefty applause. Drumaestro offers enough solos to please the most avid fan, but doesn't monopolize the show. He spotlights his talented, versatile sidemen in a number of solos of their own to share the evening's honors. The near capacity audience was with Krupa all the way.

Jose
Variety
June 3, 1970

The Plaza 9 (New York) is ending its season with Gene Krupa making one of his infrequent appearances. He hasn't had a regular combo for some time, and for this engagement has taken a crew of tooters, with saxist-trumpeter Eddie Shu as the lead musician, and turned over virtually the entire proceedings to him. Krupa was at one time the leading figure of the skins—his virtuosity was so great that he popularized the drum solos. He still shows that skill, even though the vigor of a former era has diminished. He spent his time lately giving anti-narco lectures before youthful audiences. Krupa weaves winning patterns on the drum setup. This trip in, he seems to prefer softer brush work and cymbals during his backgrounding. However, his stick thumping still shows evidence of his innovating endowments. At the Plaza 9, he is working before an audience of appreciators and rememberers. They comprise a set of solid folk, many of whom are presumably reliving their early days when Krupa was at his height, and as they were too. There were vocal huzzahs at the conclusion of his first set. Shu is a versatile musician who takes over the major exposition of the music at the outset. He's backed by Scott Holt at the bass and Dick Wellstood at the piano. It's a lively group, albeit drawing old-fashioned musical figures. In that way, they fit in with the lead musical figure and the audience. There's as much applause for them as there is for Krupa.

Gene Krupa

"THE
BASIS
OF JAZZ"

CHAPTER TEN

THE BASIS OF JAZZ

by Gene Krupa, as told to George T. Simon, Metronome Magazine/July, 1954

The Basis Of Jazz published in conjunction with the opening of the Gene Krupa-Cozy Cole Drum School

The late and great Dave Tough once wrote a funny thing in his Metronome column that still made an awful lot of sense. I can't remember it word for word, but it went something like this:

A reader wrote in, asking what was the basic requisite for becoming a good drummer. The most important thing, replied Davey, is to have a good beat. If you don't have a good beat, you might as well give up before you start and become a plumber.

Of course, he went on, if you find you can't make it as a plumber either, then there's only one thing left to do, and that's to become a recording supervisor. This consists merely of sitting in a glass-enclosed booth, and when the trumpets are blowing woefully sharp, you come rushing out of your control room yelling, "Too much brushes! Too much brushes!"

I have no comment to offer about recording supervisors, but I do feel that unless a person has at least a modicum of talent he should forget trying to become a musician. Once he does start to become one, though, he should learn all that he can about his instrument. Because playing jazz is so wrapped up in emotions, naturally musicians play better when they feel good. But a musician with a well-developed technique, who knows how and why he does things, stands less of a chance of having an off night simply because his basic technique will permit him to perform at least the fundamentals, if nothing else.

There are, of course, some outstanding musicians — or I should say drummers, because I know more whereof I speak in that department — who, without the benefit of studying, are invariably great both as musicians and as entertainers. The two Rays, Bauduc and McKinley, are consistently fine drummers, who, because of their experience and, of course, their immense basic talent, never let you down. And then there is Buddy Rich, to me the greatest drummer of all time, bar none. Buddy was brought up on the drums; be started playing them professionally when he was just a kid, and he has been developing ever since. Actually, I wouldn't be surprised if studying might hurt him, because Buddy is both the most natural and the most uninhibited drummer I've ever heard, and if he tried to figure out how and why he did certain things, he might lose some of that amazing freedom that characterizes his work.

Buddy, though, is an exception. The rest of the top drummers today have all studied and benefitted thereby. Louie Bellson not only knows his drums, he knows his music, as his great arrangements for the Duke prove. Cozy Cole, my partner in our new drum school, has studied at Julliard and must know his instrument mighty well — or else how would he be able to teach it so well? Don Lamond and Specs Powell, two more who come quickly to mind, are not only great swing drummers, but are good enough to hold down top studio jobs, where they have to play just about everything at sight.

I'd like to think that we could pay the same sort of compliment to all of the younger musicians who are coming up these days, but, from what I've heard, I'm afraid that some of them have not studied their instruments the way they should. Yes, most of them can blow good jazz passages, but when it comes to trying other things they're stymied by lack of adequate technique. It's a funny thing, the difference between what you can expect from musicians today and back in the thirties when Benny's band was at its height. I remember then that when Benny took on a new musician, it was just taken for granted that he could read well and play in tune. The big question then used to be, "Can he swing?" Today, you take it for granted that a new musician plays jazz, but you can't always be sure that he knows how to handle his instrument.

Which brings me to probably my biggest gripe of all. That's the tendency on the part of musicians, both young and old, to put down other musicians not because of how well they do or do not play, but because of the vein in which they play. The thing to consider when judging any musician is not what you think of the type of music he is playing, but rather how well he is playing whatever type he is attempting to play.

One thing that I don't think that many young musicians give the older jazz musicians credit for is the fact that they were the ones who conceived things, and that they didn't just listen to a lot of records and copy and perhaps make a few changes. To me, one of the most exciting things that happened in my younger days was when I heard Vic Berton, the drummer with Arnold Johnson's band, play triplets, really fast, on a top cymbal. I just couldn't figure out how a man could play that fast with one hand till he let me in on the secret. He had conceived the idea of holding a coin in his left hand, and using it underneath the cymbal as he was holding it. Today, when I mention Berton's ingenuity to kids, they just shrug their shoulders and say, "So what?"

It's because of men like Vic Berton and the tricks and shortcuts they discovered that today's young musicians are better equipped technically. But why shouldn't they be? Look at the head start those trailblazers have given them. The kids should be thankful.

On the other hand, those of us who are no longer kids, should not just rest on our laurels — provided, of course, we have any to rest on. The concepts of time are quite different nowadays, and it's more than just conceivable that the kind of time you admired and learned to play ten years ago would lose you a job in a modern band today.

Here again, technique plays an important part, because the well-schooled drummer should have enough technique at his command to adapt his playing to almost any style. I won't say that a drummer who just can't feel modern time will ever be able to play it, but I will say that, all things being equal, the drummer who has learned his fundamentals well stands a much better chance of restyling his work simply because he is able to recognize, from a purely mechanical viewpoint, what modern drummers are doing, and because he has enough command of his drums to beat out at least a rough copy of what he has analyzed.

Cozy and I, as you may know, have started a drum school called the Krupa-Cole Drum School, and our main reason for doing this, outside of wanting a business of our own, is to try to turn out more musicianly drummers. Because of our experience we are able to teach all phases of drumming, and the gratifying part of it is that each of us has learned a lot from the other, and, at the same time, while teaching, each of us has relearned some of the things which we had forgotten about.

Another reason we are anxious to turn out good drummers is because we want other musicians to respect our instrument more. Some time back, drummers used to be put in the class of brooms, sort of the janitors of the band. Today, though, a good drummer is as important as any other musician in the band, though I must say — and here comes another gripe of mine — that you can't often prove that point by the arrangements drummers are forced to play. I do wish — and I think I echo the sentiments of many drummers — that musicians who want to arrange would get a better knowledge of drums. I'm sure that if they wrote more comprehensive drum parts, they would be much more apt to hear the sounds which they want to hear, but which, because of inadequate drum writing, they too often don't hear.

I think this sloppy attitude on the part of arrangers toward drummers is at least partly a carry over from the days when a drummer who read was automatically put down as a non-swinger. As I pointed out earlier, that just isn't true anymore.

With jazz getting more and more complicated all the time, drummers just have to learn how to read and play different beats. Most of the top drummers today are pretty intelligent guys. What's more, if you'll stop to examine them more closely, you'll find that they are pretty down-to-earth humans. I recently played a jazz concert which featured several drummers, and I just say I felt very proud not only because they performed so well — all of them were obviously well-schooled — but also because their deportment was so excellent. I don't mean to sound like a Sunday School teacher, but, let's face it, we could use a lot of good deportment on the part of musicians these days, and so when a lot of it comes all at one time from a group of drummers — well, you can't exactly blame me for feeling proud to be associated with them, can you!

I think it all boils down to something that's true in all phases of life, namely, that the well-schooled, studious artist has enough self-confidence to carry him through almost any given set-up; that he no longer needs to resort to all sorts of extraneous devices to draw attention to himself and to build up his ego. A thorough musician knows he's good; he doesn't feel the need to become a character. If only for that reason alone, I believe wholeheartedly that plenty of studying of whatever you are trying to do is just about the greatest investment a person can make.

GENE KRUPA/

BUDDY RICH

INTERVIEW

CHAPTER ELEVEN

GENE KRUPA/BUDDY RICH INTERVIEW

Willis Conover/interviewer broadcast over **Voice of America Radio** Printed in **Metronome Magazine,** March/April, 1956

Conover: On today's program we're going to compare the work of two of the world's greatest and most famous drummers: Buddy Rich, whose fame is not limited to his drumming, but also (extends) to his orchestras and to his work as a dancer, a singer, and an all-round entertainer; and Gene Krupa, who, of course, has not only been a drummer in other men's orchestras, but has been a leader of his own orchestra, one of the world's finest, which has introduced many of the great stars we all recognize today. To begin our survey of Gene Krupa, let's go back to the Carnegie Hall Jazz Concert in which Gene Krupa soloed and starred with the Benny Goodman Orchestra. Gene, I suppose this was a tremendous occasion to look forward to when the Goodman band finally made the hallowed halls of Carnegie Hall.

Krupa: *It was a pretty big thrill, Willis. I never thought I'd be able to buy my way into the front door, much less the stage door. It was pretty great. Loved it.*

Conover: And how many times did you return to Carnegie Hall in the Goodman Orchestra?

Krupa: *Oh, that's like...oh, with the Goodman Orchestra. Just that one time; but I've been there many, many times since with Jazz At The Phil.*

Conover: Jazz At The Philharmonic has been an unusual experience, for, I suppose, everyone who has joined the Norman Granz troupe.

Krupa: *Yes, I'd say it's about the best job in the world today (chuckling).*

Conover: Do you feel happier starring with the other great stars, rather than leading your own orchestra? Or is there a mixed emotion there, Gene?

Krupa: *Well, I guess I like variety pretty much, but I do enjoy this work very much. Particularly with Buddy on the gig, we get a chance to knock each other out. It's just wonderful.*

Conover: Well, do you want to set the stage for the famous performance of *Sing, Sing, Sing*?

Krupa: *Introduce the guys in the band, or what?*

Conover: Why don't you speak of the guys in the band and also your impressions as the curtains opened and you saw the audience out front and you realized what could happen.

Krupa: *Uh-huh...well...uh...let's see, the guys in the band were Harry James and Ziggy Elman, Chris Griffin, Murray McEachern, Vernon Brown, Jess Stacy, Lionel Hampton, Teddy Wilson, Hymie Schertzer, Adrian — not Adrian — uh...*

Conover: Arthur.

Krupa: *Arthur Rollini. Uh...gee, I th-Billy Depew, I think on saxophone. I can't remember the other guys, but that's enough, right there. Uh, I guess we started off a bit shaky. If I remember correctly, the first tune was "Don't Be That Way," but the one you are going to listen to now, we're into it already and the nerves more or less have worn off. So, uh, here it is, "Sing, Sing, Sing."*

Conover: Gene, how did it feel when you finally left Goodman and formed your own orchestra? Was there a sort of shakiness about invading the bandleadership field?

Krupa: *No...I felt pretty confident, I guess as a result of the sales talks all the various agencies gave me, and they showed me big fat contracts and everything, so it was, uh...I wasn't too scared about that really.*

Conover: I know you made a point of getting the finest stars around to work with you.

Krupa: *Yes, I've had some pretty good luck finding wonderful talent. Just a few of 'em, the musicians are Roy Eldridge, Charlie Ventura, Vido Musso, Sam Donahue, Charlie Kennedy, Red Rodney — oh, I could go on for a long time. Some of the better singers were Anita O'Day, Johnny*

Desmond, Dave Lambert, Buddy Stewart, and of course the arrangers who were largely responsible for a wonderful book, were Jimmy Mundy, and, uh, Neal Hefti, Benny Carter, George Williams and Gerry Mulligan.

Conover: How many sides have you put out as a bandleader? Have you ever counted them up, Gene?

Krupa: *Good gosh, I never counted, but I guess about three or four hundred.*

Conover: Well, let's try one of the swinginest. Gene Krupa and his Orchestra, *Leave Us Leap,* (As record begins, Gene says, *Gee, I forgot to mention Eddie Finckel!*)

(Buddy Rich joins discussion)

Conover: Gene, what was the first time that you heard Buddy play?

Krupa: *Uh...actually, I heard Buddy play when he joined Tommy Dorsey's orchestra in — I don't know exactly when he joined, but this was in, I'd say, 1939. At the Palmer House in Chicago. And the only reason I didn't hear him before then was I was scared to death. Because the guys in Goodman's band — like Harry James and all the chaps — used to come by and say, "Man, this kid over at the Hickory House is going to scare you to death. Wait 'til you hear him."*

I'm often asked the question, particularly since I've gone into the drum school business, along with Cozy Cole, we have a studio in New York — I'm very often asked "How about natural talent against studied technique and so forth?" Well, I've watched everybody rather closely, and there are three giants in the drum world, and of these three Buddy stands out head and shoulders. They are Buddy Rich, Ray Bauduc, and Ray McKinley. When I speak of natural drummers I'm talking about guys that are playing with the talent God gave 'em. But here's an amazing thing. While this isn't true of either Ray — McKinley or Bauduc — it's true of Buddy. You can watch Buddy play and actually if you watch him, you'd think he's the most studied person in the world. And even Buddy himself will make something — like, we'll be in the dressing room, he'll pick up a pair of sticks and say: "Well, what is this?" And he'll rattle a little bit and actually, if I break it down, get him to do it slow enough, I can name it. I can break it down into whatever it is. And inherently, naturally, he fingers all these things correctly. Now, I know why this is.

But let me tell you something. No doubt when he was a young child—he doesn't remember this, he told me himself—when he was a young child and standing around for his daddy to rehearse his act and things in the old vaudeville days, well, those old pit drummers were just wonderful. Every one of 'em. Well, now y'know, this little kid standing around? He's got to absorb all these things. That's how come the wonderful left hand. That's how come the great ambidexterity which is absolutely necessary for a good drummer. To me he's the greatest.

Conover: Buddy, what's your rebuttal to that? Or is there? Is "rebuttal" the word?

Rich: Well, now, you put me in a very embarrassing position. I don't know **how** to answer a thing like that. That's probably the greatest compliment that has **ever** been paid me by anyone, especially when it comes from such a giant as Gene. Because, as anyone knows, anybody that knows anything about drums — and this is not going to sound like an Alphonse and Gaston type reply — uh...Gene is absolutely the first man when it comes to drums. The inspiration for every big-name drummer in the band business today, I think. I think at one time every drummer in the business today, at one time wanted to play like Krupa or wanted to win a Gene Krupa drum contest. This is the big inspiration for drummers and naturally it has to be the same way with me. After hearing Gene with Benny for so many years and listening to the recordings and everything, uh, this is the guy the kids want to play like more than anybody else. And just like anybody else the same goes for me. This is my man and, uh, you can't **say** any more. This is the President. And, uh, that's it.

Conover: Well, how do you agree with Gene's definition of intuitive or natural drummers as against trained or studied drummers?

Rich: Well...(laughs)

Conover: He has put you in the "natural" drum class.

Rich: I'm a lucky one see? I think — and I think Gene will agree — I think to be an expert at anything, I think the best thing to do is to study. I've tried, but I'm too stupid. I can't sit down long enough to absorb any kind of learning. At one time I wanted to play like Lionel Hampton. I went out and bought myself a set of vibraphones and hired a great teacher, and after about three weeks I never saw the vibraphones again because I just couldn't absorb the things I was being taught. But I think any young drummer starting out today definitely should get himself a great teacher and learn all there is to know about the instrument that he wants to play.

Conover: Well, do you agree with Gene's selection — excluding yourself, out of modesty of course — of the greatest drummers today or the greatest drummers of the past?

Rich: Definitely. I think Bauduc is one of the truly great drummers and of course McKinley rates right along with him. But Gene left out two...

Krupa: *Mm.*

All: (Laughs)

Rich: He left out two of my boys and I'm sure they're his boys, too.

Conover: Can I see if I can name them, 'cause you've never mentioned this before?

Rich: (Laughs). Go ahead.

Conover: I would say Jo Jones and Sid Catlett. Now maybe I'm wrong.

Rich: Well, Sid Catlett of **course** deserves to be in that company. But he left out CH — the daddy of 'em all.

(Krupa and Rich laugh)

Rich: Chick Webb! But of course Jo Jones. My all star poll for drummers would be Gene, Jo Jones, Chick Webb, McKinley, Bauduc and Catlett. Those...everybody had a distinctive style, and certainly great technique, and they could sure swing a band.

Conover: Well, since both of you were, uh, already in the prime before many of the young drummers of some of the new movements in jazz came along, uh, you've been in a good position to get an opinion of how the drummers such — well I won't mention names because I don't know what your answers are going to be, but how those drummers compare both with the drummers **before** — or who were **established** before — and also in relationship to the music that they're playing today.

Krupa: *Mm-hmm. Well, Willis, I'd say that the "new music" actually hasn't found itself enough yet to...to...to showcase a drummer. Do you agree with that case Bud?*

Rich: Well, I don't even think, uh—I don't want to get into this discussion because...

Krupa: (Laughs)

Rich: I have definite and very set opinions about the so-called modern school of music and drummers. Whereas in the days when it was necessary to swing a band, where a drummer had to be a powerhouse, today more or less the "cool school" has taken over, and I don't believe there's such a thing as a "cool drummer." You either swing a band or don't swing a band and that's what's lacking today. There aren't any guys around who get back there and play with any kind of guts. And I like a heavyweight. I'm not a flyweight. I like—in my fighting, I like heavyweights and in my music I like emotionally good, strong heavyweight type of jazz. And it's just lacking today.

Conover: Well, how do you feel about the idea of drums used almost as a melody instrument rather just as a rhythmic instrument?

Rich: Well, it would be very nice if you could play a melody on it. But primarily, the drummer's supposed to sit back there and swing the band. Am I right?

Krupa: *Yeah. If you're going to start with melody you'll need some tympani, I think.*

Rich: (Laughs). And some tunable tom-toms.

Both: (Laugh).

Krupa: *That's right.*

Rich: I think the drummer should sit back there and play some drums, and never mind about the tunes. Just get up there and wail behind whoever is sitting up there playing the solo. And this is what is lacking, definitely lacking in music today.

Krupa: *Well, that's Buddy's big...big tip. I mean, uh, he can play so hard, and yet make a sound, rather than a, a, a noise.*

Conover: Well, how do you set up these drum battles? Because we'd like to hear one of your performances together at a Jazz At The Philharmonic...

Krupa: *Well, you know the nice thing about it? They're not set up!*

Conover: There's no agreement in advance?

Rich: No. (laughs)

Krupa: *No. We get up there and we wail. I don't think two nights have been alike yet.*

Rich: No.

Krupa: (Laughs).

Rich: And they never will be because then it would get to be kind of stiff, boring kind of thing. I think we get up on the stand every night and we look at each other and you listen to all the comments that come at you from the audience. Naturally, they're partisan groups and they're all shouting for their favorites, and we sit down at the drums and we laugh, and some nights Gene'll start a tempo or other nights I'll start the tempo. And we just start to **play**. And some nights it's great, and other nights it's laughs, and other nights it's boring, because that's what makes — anything that's spontaneous is a — it's a free feeling. We get up there and play just exactly what we feel that particular night. When we play places like Carnegie Hall where the places are sold out we know that people are listening uh, we play good. We play other places where we don't think there's too much interest — rather than listening — I think the people would just rather be heard **themselves** — so we let **them** scream and we play **under** them.

Conover: (Laughs)

Rich: But we have...we have a ball doing it. I'm sure that Gene will say just about the same thing.

Krupa: *I'll bear you out, Bud. Sure.*

Conover: Well, let's listen to one...one of a number of drum battles, or let's say happy challenges, between Gene Krupa and Buddy Rich at the drums. Gene and Buddy, it's been a pleasure having you with us for the full hour today.

Rich: Well, it's been a great pleasure to be here with you, Willis. And we hope everybody listening enjoyed it half as much as we've enjoyed being able to sit down here and talk with you, and talk with Gene, and really get to feel **free** to express exactly what we feel about each other. It's been a kick.

Krupa: *For me, too. And I may say, Willis, that we've been out on Jazz At The Phil for two weeks now, and this is the first show we've made, and of course we'll be over across the ocean in the little bit too, and hope to see all you guys then.*

126

"THE

GENE KRUPA

STORY" 1959

CHAPTER TWELVE

THE GENE KRUPA STORY / 1959

I did the soundtracks and taught Sal (Mineo) from the soundtracks, you know, note for note. Sal was very diligent and had his parts down pat. To begin with, I thought Sal did a wonderful job. It's one thing to record and shoot at the same time. That's easy enough. But to have to play to someone else's soundtracks, even to play to your own soundtracks, is very, very tough. And Sal did very well.

I had to leave for another engagement before the music had been written for several of the closing titles (and the main titles and stuff), so the musical director told me what he had in mind—it would go something like this or that—and I just put a click track on and made the drum parts. Then, after the music had been written, the conductor put the drum parts on and added the music. Had I not worked with a metronome and been accustomed to working with one or the other, I would have been up a tree. But I had no trouble staying with this click track. You set it for whatever tempo you want and that is it...I'm waiting to see "The Benny Goodman Story." I never did see that one.

I thought the movie could have been better. See, at that time, in films, realism wasn't too prevalent. They had to pretty everything up, you know. And I think they did it the way they thought I would have liked it to have been. But if they merely did it the way it was, it could have been a great picture.

REVIEWS/ *THE GENE KRUPA STORY*

John Tynan
down beat
Magazine,
February 4, 1960

Just when it seemed that Hollywood was ready to produce a really mature and intelligent motion picture on a jazzman's life, along comes *The Gene Krupa Story* and we're back where we started — with *Syncopation* in 1941.

But perhaps the comparison with *Syncopation* is unfair. At least that picture, for all its nonsense, had some moments of valid musical interest. The only musically interesting moments in this purported story of Krupa's life are to be found in Leith Stevens' spare but effective underscore. The rest of the music in the picture is tired and unimaginative, well played by the crack studio orchestra but far from inspiring.

The story line hinges on things irrelevant to Krupa's music, his break from the Roman Catholic seminary where he studied for the priesthood, and a proclivity for smoking marijuana. These facets of the man's life may have been thought to make for good drama, but emphasis on them in the picture only distorts and detracts from Krupa's real importance as the first jazz drummer to win an international fan following and blaze a new trail in his art.

As Gene Krupa, the drummer, actor Mineo achieves remarkable on-camera synchronization with Gene's soundtrack recording; as Krupa the man, Sal plays the perennial juvenile, a pouting babyface who could not have lasted a week in the rough-and-tumble band days of the twenties and thirties.

As for the plot line, it's a simple case of the facts be damned. For dramatic purposes, Krupa is saddled with a tag-along trumpet-playing buddy, Eddie Sirota (convincingly played by James Darren) and a girl- next-door in the person of Susan Kohner, who becomes an appealing Ethel Maguire. For the rest, fiction is piled upon fiction.

In real life, Krupa came to New York with Red McKenzie; in the film he goes on his own hook with only his buddy and girlfriend to hold his drumsticks. No mention is made of his extensive jazz background in Chicago during 1927-28, or of his recording debut in that city, December 7, 1927, with the McKenzie-Condon Chicagoans, a colorful group of hell-raisers the injection of which into the story could only have enhanced the period atmosphere. Instead we are given the impression that Krupa's Chicago days were taken up with teenage hi-jinks bearing no relation to serious playing.

But the most hilarious goof—if a slightly macabre one—occurs during a party at Krupa's lavish apartment after the drummer had joined the Goodman band and is established as a top sideman in his profession. (For the historically minded, let it be noted that Gene joined Goodman in 1935.) At the height of the festivities, three individuals enter. They are introduced as Tommy Dorsey (adequately played by Bobby Troup), Frankie Trumbauer and Bix Biederbecke! Bix died August 7, 1931.

There appear a flock of other absurdities, such as the prominent on-camera display of interracial bands during a period when the presence of Negroes in white bands was restricted to the presence of Teddy Wilson and Lionel Hampton in the Goodman band. But an unforgivable oversight lies in the treatment accorded Roy Eldridge and Anita O'Day. Eldridge is simply ignored as a figure in the Krupa saga: no mention whatever is made of this jazz giant and catalyst in Krupa's career; it is as if he never existed. Anita is fleetingly presented singing *Memories of You* during a party scene in Krupa's apartment and identified almost by accident by Krupa's femme fatale.

The less said the better about sequences concerning Krupa's introduction to and subsequent arrest for possession of marijuana. Not only is the subject matter handled in a ridiculously juvenile and melodramatic fashion, it insults the intelligence to boot. Benny Goodman never appears in the picture, due to financial circumstances beyond the control of the producer. But Tommy Dorsey figures disproportionately in the story, as does Dave Tough (surprisingly well played by Shelly Manne), and Red Nichols, looking not a day older than he currently is, is seen and heard in a jam session scene placed roughly about 1930.

There was an excellent opportunity here for a worthwhile film-story of a great jazzman's life and times. Too bad screenwriter Orin Jannings didn't realize that.

Movies on TV, edited by Steven H. Scheuer

Corny, highly fictionalized account of the rise to fame by drummer Gene Krupa. One of the worst scenes is a bit of hokum which describes how Krupa got in with a fast crowd and stated smoking marijuana. The casting of Sal Mineo as Krupa is another stroke of idiocy.

Leonard Feather, *The New Edition of the Encyclopedia of Jazz*

...Allegedly based on the drummer's life. Ludicrously inaccurate even by Hollywood standards, it neglected most of the salient facts and consisted largely of anachronisms, distortions and outright fiction.

David Meeker, *Jazz in the Movies*

Reasonably straightforward Columbia screen biography of the drummer, conventionally scripted but beautifully played and cast, particularly by Sal Mineo in the title role, who works wonders matching his movements to Krupa's own soundtrack drumming.

Clive Hirschhorn, *The Hollywood Musical*

Though far too young for the role, Sal Mineo played drummer Gene Krupa...and was never really convincing as Krupa the heavy drinker and Krupa the habitual marijuana smoker. Following the familiar pattern of the idealistic young musician, who, after deserting his wholesome upbringing and the priesthood, for the more exciting world of jazz, goes through a rough patch, but bounced back, etc., etc. It was a solid but uninspired effort which relied more on its musical sequences than its screenplay.

PRIMARY SOURCES:

1) Interview with Robert Tiles, **Music Journal,** May, 1967.

2) Interview with Gene Webb, **down beat Magazine,** published March 14, 1974

Gene Krupa

SLOWING DOWN

SLOWING DOWN

March, 1959

down beat Magazine, March 5, 1959

I daresay I've mellowed a bit. I'd probably liken myself to a pitcher who used to throw very hard, didn't want to get out of the game, and started to pitch with his bean instead of his arm...I certainly have to go along with progress, but it has to be presented carefully and intelligently. I like any kind of music ably performed. I respect the musicians. But I can't go for the music just because it's a certain type. Sometimes you get too far out and you're liable to lose them. Benny's stuff will never die...When I'm at home in Yonkers and have the time, I go downstairs before dinner and practice. I put the metronome at a good fast clip and try to keep up with it. I have a complete set of tympanies and just about everything that has been written for the drum...more than 100 scores and books.

March, 1962

down beat Magazine, March 29, 1962

I work only 19 weeks a year. And 18 of those weeks are spent at the Metropole in New York and the remaining week at the Steel Pier in Atlantic City. This schedule permits me to be at home with my wife, to take care of chores around the house, and to practice and experiment, all of which were next to impossible during my traveling years.

Don't misunderstand...my taste for playing has not dulled. I'm still deeply involved with drums, but you can't fly at a fast pace forever. A time comes when you stop and take stock. After my heart attack (November, 1960), I came to the realization that, considering my situation and the condition of the music business, I would do well to cool a bit and concentrate on several things I had been putting off for years.

I do enjoy it (working with a quartet), though I feel more responsibility in a large band. And after all, small bands are what the public is buying today. It doesn't seem likely that the big bands will come back. But you never know, perhaps the Twist will create an interest in dance bands again. As for my putting together another big band...No, I don't think I could make that one-nighter grind, or the five-shows-a-day theater routine. I'll stick with this set-up for personal appear- ances and leave my big-band playing for record dates.

My style hasn't changed too much. I still play on the drums rather than leaning heavily on the cymbals. Unlike the modern guys, I keep the bass drum going. I feel the big drum should be used to keep time and for accents. But I must admit that certain things I've heard Art Blakey, Shelly Manne, and Max Roach do have found their way into my repertoire. And often I incorporate some of the modern things to accommodate the youngsters in my group.

My job, however, remains the same — to keep time, to extract appropriate, supporting sounds from the instrument, to be a musician.

December, 1965

---

down beat Magazine, December 2, 1965

I'm playing with more assurance today than I ever had. I think you can compare me to an old-time pitcher who has lost his fast ball; he pitches more with his head than with his arm. I play differently today than I did 20 years ago. When younger, I'd break 24 pairs of drumsticks a week — and break 12 drumheads a year. Now I've mellowed. Hell, I've grown older. I only go through 10 pairs of sticks a week and I can't remember when I broke my last head. Why should I want to quit? Frankly, what else could I do? I like to play; I like to meet people; I just plain like the music business...I never have played with a symphony orchestra. Since I was a kid I always wanted to play with a symphony. I once had a chance to do something with the Boston Pops, and there was even talk I might work something out with the New York Philharmonic. But I've either been too busy to make good on an offer, or I haven't had an offer when I had the time. Before I call it quits, I would like to make it just once.

Fall, 1967, upon announcing retirement

I felt too lousy to play and I was sure I sounded lousy.

March, 1972

down beat Magazine, published March 14, 1974

Buddy (Rich) has been ill lately, and I haven't been too well, either. That's the reason for my semi-retirement. Louis Bellson took over Buddy's band. They asked me to do it, too, but I couldn't accept, (any more than) perhaps for a night or two. I'm just too old to take it for a week or anything like that. I intend to go on as I am now. I don't want to push it. I do, say, four or five gigs a month, concerts mostly. The playing is very diversified. One night I'll work with my Quartet and the next I'll work with a big band. Then the third night I'll do some traditional jazz playing, you know, with the Chicago guys, and, of course, I'm going to start doing some clinics.

September, 1972

International Musician, September 1972

I never felt more like playing in my entire life. But I have to cool it and follow a reasonable schedule. I'm still trying to learn. It's an endless process. When I retired, I didn't do much except play with my kids, practice, read, watch TV and coach my local baseball team until about 18 months ago. Then I began working again but soon realized that I had to pace myself carefully. That's the way it's been. I'm hopeful things will improve. Now I manage to play a bit, lecture on the narcotics thing, make appearances for the Slingerland Drum Company, whose drums I've used for almost 40 years. Recently, I went to the Frankfurt (Germany) Trade Fair for them. I also do work for charitable causes that are meaningful to me. And I try to remain musically current. That's important. You don't have to like everything new out there. But you have to know about it. All through my life, I've listened, adapted if I thought it right and necessary. That's what happened in the late forties, when I had the modern band. I learned from the young cats and they from me. It's still happening. I'm just sorry I can't be more active. But as the manager of the Steel Pier in Atlantic City used to say to me: "Gene, you work too hard. Really you should rest, take things a big easier." At long last I'm taking his advice.

Gene Krupa

138

GENE KRUPA
ON
DRUMMERS

GENE KRUPA ON DRUMMERS

Metronome Magazine, October, 1943

Baby Dodds, Zutty Singleton, Tubby Hall: *These three Goliaths of the drum world are remarked about in the same breath because they entered my drum life simultaneously. It was my good luck to be weaned and raised on Baby's press roll, Zutty's "watch that tempo, Jack, give them notes their full value," (must be uttered forcibly); and Tubby's playing the amateur Charleston contest at the Sunset Cafe, Friday nights in Chicago.*

George Wettling: *Whose style was, in the old days, a pure, unadorned one, and remains beautifully so, even to this day.*

Davey Tough: *Blessed with an abundance of technique but is reluctant to show it off, content to sit back and do only what, to his mind, a drummer should do, keep good time.*

Cuba Austin: *Came my first lesson in showmanship, for which Cuba Austin was responsible. Question any musician who knew that wonderful organization (McKinney's Cotton Pickers) and be assured that Cuba played no little part in the success of the outfit from the standpoints of commercialism and musicianship.*

Chick Webb: *The most luminous of all drum stars, the master, the little giant of the big noise. For those who have never heard the Chick, I feel no small amount of compas-*

sion...*Chick gassed me, but good, on one occasion at the Savoy, in a battle with Benny's band, and I repeat now what I said then, I was never cut by a better man.*

Sonny Greer: *It would not have sounded like Duke Ellington were it not for his drummer, Sonny Greer...Any man but Greer in Greer's chair would utterly destroy the sound-color of the Ellington ensemble and that is something dearly worth preserving.*

Cozy Cole: *He's a particular favorite because he is made up of that unbeatable combination, a terrific natural talent plus the scientific knowledge acquired by intense study.*

Ray McKinley: *The man of impeccable taste...Mack has a twist all his very own on a boogie woogie riff which no one seems to be able to steal from him.*

Jo Jones: *Out of Kansas City into the big time to remain there came the Basie Band propelled by the powerful rhythmic drive of Jo Jones. On high hat cymbals Joe is without peer and truly a wizard.*

Sid Catlett: *As big as he is, Big Sidney employs a most gentle touch.*

Buddy Rich: *Truly a remarkable young man and one for whom I have sincere admiration, musically and otherwise. I like the way Buddy literally dances drums. Of the younger crop, he is, to put it mildly, outstanding. I suspect a good deal of my profound esteem for him is governed by the fact that, while he is young and performs refreshingly, there is that quality of sureness present which denotes absolute control, acquired only by long and good experience.*

down beat Magazine, March 19, 1962

Oliver Jackson: *The kid with Lionel Hampton has something. He plays with assurance and authenticity and has a fine grasp of the essentials of jazz drumming. His time is good—that's so important. Because he plays so well for others, he reminds me of a young Jo Jones.*

Joe Morello: *Excellent technique and coordination gives his work dimension. Everything he plays is crisp and well defined.*

Mel Lewis: *Has come a long way. He's one of the few working drummers who knows how to move a big band.*

down beat Magazine, December 2, 1965

Max Roach, Shelly Manne, Art Blakey: *Oh sure (they're) great. They are wonderful technicians. But I feel they still haven't developed as far musically as they will. With Buddy (Rich) it's a different thing. He's on a plateau all by himself.*

THE

MUSICIANS

ON GENE KRUPA

THE MUSICIANS ON GENE KRUPA

ANITA O'DAY
(vocalist)

In 1933 he married a telephone operator from the Dixie Hotel on 42nd Street, when that was still a theatrical center and the Dixie was a glamorous spot. But Ethel, the girl he married, wasn't all that different from a girl from his neighborhood. She really loved him and couldn't believe she'd captured this handsome cat who was obviously headed for the big time.

By 1941 Ethel wasn't around much anymore. Gene had developed a roving eye. Once after (boyfriend) Carl (Hoff) left, he even joined me in my extra seat one night. We chitchatted about music and this and that. He began to move in and very casually asked: "How would like to have breakfast with me?"

"Sorry," I told him. "I never mix business with pleasure."

"Good girl." A few minutes later, he said he guessed he'd try to get some sleep. I never had any more propositions—if it was one—from Gene. I was glad. I like Ethel.

Not that it would have made that much difference. Gene wasn't handling the temptations that go with success too well. In addition to the girls on the road, he had a little fling with Dinah Shore and then moved into the big leagues with Lana Turner. Dinah chose me as one of her ten favorite singers in a magazine layout. But I never was sure whether she admired my singing or just liked Gene and wanted to help by giving him a little indirect publicity.

Dinah had a nice figure and face that wasn't bad after the experts got done fooling around with it, but Lana had a dynamite figure and Gene didn't call her "Dreamface" for nothing.

Lana and I were on a first-name basis without really knowing one another. She had to pass my dressing room to get to Gene's. When she'd go by, she'd call out, "Hi, Anita."

"Hi, Lana."

That was it.

She hung out with Gene, not with the hired hands, although she did come to my dressing room one time to ask if she could use my make-up mirror, comb and brush. I didn't ask any questions and she didn't offer any explanations on how she got disheveled.

Eventually, Gene settled $100,000 cash on Ethel in return for a divorce. He wasn't going to mess with any paltry alimony and in 1941 or 1942 $100,000 was a sizable sum. Ethel accepted it and quietly faded from the scene. Gene's romance with Lana was in the words of a famous songwriter "too hot not to cool down." She eventually fluffed him off for someone else.

After that Gene drank more heavily and used a little pot, which eventually got him into serious trouble but made him a lot easier to work for...

We recorded *Let Me Off Uptown* at Liederkranz Hall in New York on May 8, 1941. Roy (Eldridge) was a small, round-faced black man, but he seemed ten feet tall when he took those trumpet solos. *Let Me Off Uptown* was just bits of dialogue over vamping music followed by a chorus, more dialogue and then Roy's spine-tingling trumpet solo. Gene used to tell people that with the arrival of Roy and me he felt the whole band began to find itself and really move. He also said that *Let Me Off Uptown* was the biggest hit he ever had...

Three days after my (wedding) ceremony, Carl arrived waving a newspaper and saying, "My God, Anita, guess who's been busted!"

He didn't need to tell me. A wild-man shot of Gene at the drums and being hustled into a marked police car by some burly officers took up almost the entire front page of a San Francisco newspaper Carl had bought.

The story said Gene had been charged with possession of a controlled substance and contributing to the delinquency of a minor. The minor was his valet. His valet? Gene had no valet. But when I saw the name, John Pateakos, I realized this was the replacement for our regular band boy who had been drafted. Gene had hired 17-year-old Pateakos because most adult, able-bodied men were in the service or defense work.

As Gene later told the story, the regular band boy had wanted to give him a going-away present. But surveying Gene's 15 wardrobe trunks and cashmere sweaters, silk shirts, Sulka ties and, well, you name it, the band boy went out and brought him some high-grade grass. Pleased at the thought, Gene thanked him and carelessly stuffed it into his coat pocket.

I'm not trying to convince you Gene didn't use grass on occasion. He did. But if it was a choice between grass and booze, booze won nine times out of ten.

Unfortunately, there was a headline-hunting Treasury department man in the area who found out about the gift. Knowing nothing grabbed bigger headlines than a popular star getting busted, he specialized in star-busting. So he and some local authorities showed up at the theater with a search warrant and shook Gene down. They came up empty-handed.

Gene knew that the next stop would be his hotel. So he slipped aside and quietly called the new band boy. He told him to take out the laundry and to make sure that he took the cigarettes in his coat pocket and flushed them down the toilet. Instead, the kid filched them. So the authorities nailed Gene on both counts.

The first news report didn't seem bad. Roy Eldridge was taking over the band and trying to hold it together. Gene had hired Jake Ehrlich, probably San Francisco's top attorney, to represent him, unaware that the DA hated Ehrlich and would bear down twice as heavy on his clients.

Gene entered a guilty plea on the possession charge and drew a 90-day sentence. He pleaded not guilty to contributing to the delinquency of a minor and was convicted. He appealed...

What has never been told until now is that a good thing came out of the arrest. Gene's ex, Ethel, had never stopped loving Gene. When she read in the paper that the band had folded when headed by Roy and that Gene was about to lose his Yonkers home, she flew to San Francisco to visit him.

It wasn't easy at first. But after they'd both cried a little, Ethel asked Gene whether he remembered the hundred grand he'd settled on her at the time of their divorce. "You know, I didn't need that money," she told him, "I went back to being a telephone operator." Then she opened her purse and took out a check for $100,000 and said, "Gene, I want you to have this back. No strings attached."

I think that was when Gene grew up emotionally. He'd made his success very young and he hadn't been able to handle it. But when Ethel came to him in jail and laid that money on him, it showed real caring. He'd tossed her out, like old trash in the alley, and still she came through with that kind of devotion. I'm happy to say that Ethel's noble attitude was rewarded, because when he got out of jail he remarried her...

Unfortunately, the scandal forced Gene out of the band business. He retreated to his home in Yonkers where he fumed and raged against his fate until he broke out in a series of rashes. But finally, recognizing his impotence to do anything about his predicament, he once again embraced religion. So out of all the bad came a great good...

Gene was as magnetic as a movie star, filled with wild exuberance as his raven-colored hair, flashing brown eyes and black suit contrasted with the snow-white marnie pearl drums that surrounded him. His gum-chewing, facial gymnastics, tossing of broken sticks to the audience and general flamboyance visually complemented the Krupa sound that incorporated rolls, flams and paradiddles that reverberated throughout the theater...

People who bad-mouthed him as only a showman with a faltering beat were dead wrong most of the time. When he was paying attention to business, he had a driving beat that propelled the band.

The following comments appeared in the down beat Magazine
Gene Krupa Tribute, issued, December 6, 1973

ROY HAYNES (drummer)

He was such a wonderful person. He was so different from some other drummers I had known. Later on when I was with (Stan) Getz, we played the Tropicana in Las Vegas. Gene was doing a radio interview, and the bass player with us had heard it. Gene had talked so much about me on the show. That was very inspiring. He was a wonderful person and a great master of the instrument.

SONY STITT (saxophonist)

Beautiful cat, great man. I loved him. He was compatible to the music. Jazz is jazz, the way I look at it.

MAX ROACH (drummer)

A gentle and wonderful human being. The kind of exposure that he had given the instrument kind of opened the door for people to look at people like Chick Webb. I think that's very important. He was more than just another student of Black music like most of the folks are. He was also a contributor.

BOBBY SCOTT (composer/vocalist/pianist)

...I thought of our first get-together in the half-lit Basin Street night club, when he hired me to play in the new Quartet. He casually looked me over, heard me play and made a few comments about my youth. It was his affable way that relaxed me. He was self-deprecating. He talked about his "old" style of playing and how he hoped it wouldn't bore us young chaps too much. Actually, his playing never did bother me. In fact, I found it, in most cases, pleasurable. He did have trouble with bursitis, from time to time, but I don't ever remember it stopping him cold. He generally lowered the cymbals and sat higher on his stool. I was always amazed at his capacity not to make much of himself. He praised Buddy Rich and Art Blakey. He expressed interest in young players and arrangers, and it was genuine.

During one long job in Las Vegas, he bought a phonograph and a stack of serious albums and he introduced me to the music of Frederick Delius. In my studies I hadn't ever heard any Delius. The Old Man's judgement of Delius, of his originality, was right on the mark. He seemed to lean toward the Impressionists. Ravel and Debussy, the pictorial music of the early Vaughn and Delius, they all delighted him. He encouraged me to write and sing. At that time I thought of myself as a player. In his way he changed that.

...I remember how he loved his dogs and how they'd jump all over him. He could hardly get into the house with five or six of them blocking the door! The bag of silver dollars he accrued in Vegas, to bring home for the neighborhood kids. The delight he got when I found, bought and presented him with any new Thomas Merton book. The easy way he could take a rib. I never let him forget those monogrammed shorts! He took it. The ritual he always went through when I brought him one of my recorded efforts. He refused to accept the album, unless I autographed it!

...We had some wonderful times together. Eddie Shu, Whitey Mitchell, myself and the Old Man all seemed to get along easily. I think the Old Man's ease created the right kind of atmosphere. I was never criticized once by the Old Man about my playing. Our rehearsals were minimum, very short and to the point. We simply formed a piece and assigned sections to each other. We all had a say. That's how the Old Man wanted it. Most importantly, it worked. There was very little personal griping. I only once received a caution from "Ace," as I kiddingly called him, about a battle I had with a bottle!

I guess I could sum up the Old Man, simply by saying he was a gentle man. The real kind. I was impressed by how Lester Young and Roy Eldridge felt about him on purely personal basis. He was a very likable person. His friends were legion. He once told me the hardest thing in life is to live with success, to mellow. It couldn't have been easy for him. Moments of tragedy had marked his life. The losses were sometimes greater than the gains. But he did gain that most marvelous of all possessions, equanimity.

The following comments appeared in Modern Drummer Magazine's *Gene Krupa Tribute,* **issue, October/November, 1979.**

DON OSBORNE (drummer)

Gene had continuity to everything that he played. He was a very musical drummer. He played everything that fit into what was happening.

ROY C. KNAPP (drummer/teacher)

There is not a professional drummer, percussionist or other instrumentalist who does not in some way owe something and should be grateful to Gene Krupa for his imaginative and creative contributions in the modern drum techniques and styles in performance that we are using today. He invented and gave to the world a "new look" into the progressive studies in the modern rhythmic patterns for the drums, hi-hat, cymbals, wire brushes, tom-toms, tympani, mallet-played instruments and accessories. With Gene's unusual talent and the magnitude of his influence, the reaction became monumental internationally.

PETER CRISS (drummer, formerly of KISS)

He was my idol. I got to talk to him and he really liked me. He gave me lessons for about six months. He was great to take the time out to teach me. He once said to me. "You got it kid, you really got it. I've never seen anyone who wants it so bad, so I'll take the time out to teach you." Today when I do a drum solo I have that *Drum Boogie* sound and nobody uses it. The kids go wild but it's not original. I'm doing something that was done in 1935.

COZY COLE (drummer)

Gene Krupa was responsible for making the drums a solo instrument.

LIONEL HAMPTON (vibraphonist/drummer/pianist/bandleader)

I have to call Gene a miracle drummer boy. I compare him with the drummer playing the Spirit of '76. I put Gene in the category of not only a great musician and one of the worlds greatest performing artists, but he was also a real patriot. All the kids used to hear him play and he had a rapport with them that no other drummer had. The people responded to him and saw him in a different light. They never compared him to other drummers. There was always a special, honorable place for Gene. Other drummers came before him, but when Gene appeared on the scene, he mapped out a place for himself and became well-respected. It was a great thrill playing with Gene. He was always my favorite.

JIM CHAPIN (drummer/teacher/author)

Like the best of them, he was able to concentrate on his music and he meant what he played. Though his performances were visually dramatic, the sound of his music was dramatic as well. Gene was larger than life, a charismatic figure that made the public fully conscious of drummers. He was so important, it's almost difficult to talk about him.

BUDDY RICH (drummer/bandleader)

notes to **Krupa and Rich** (Verve), 1956

In 1939, I first met Gene. I started at the Hickory House in 1938. So Gene and I had been friends for years. Well, where do you begin? Gene Krupa was the beginning and the end of all jazz drummers. He's a great genius, a truly great genius of the drums. Gene discovered things that could be done with the drums that hadn't been done before, ever. He discovered these things and made the most of them. I'll tell you about Gene. Before Gene, the drums were in the background, just a part of the band. To put it in plainer terms, the drums didn't have much meaning. Along comes Gene and the drums take on meaning and they're out of the background. The drummer becomes somebody, you know? Gene gets credit for making people aware of the drummer, of what he's doing and why he's doing it, and he deserves every bit of credit. Can you imagine jazz without Gene?

NORMAN GRANZ (record producer/concert promoter)

down beat Magazine, January 25, 1952

I'll never be able to say enough for him or about him. Frankly, I was worried at first about him (when he first joined the Jazz At The Philharmonic tour in 1952). Face it. Gene is a top cat to the public. He's like Louis and Benny. Tops. So I figured maybe he'd be a great attraction, yes, but, you know, a little temperamental. Well, I'd play ball. I said, "Gene, you want to take a plane or travel alone or anything, go ahead." He laughed and said, *What for, Norm? I'm no better than anyone else.* What happened all through the tour was that Gene did anything I wanted him to do. And all the other cats are nuts about him. And I think, honestly, that they play better with his beat because they like him so much personally. As for Buddy Rich, finally, I reached the end of my patience with that guy. He was through, period. I wouldn't have him around, that's all.

ELVIN JONES (drummer/bandleader)

down beat Magazine, December 15, 1977

*Sing, Sing, Sing...*is another piece I could never play, but I can always appreciate Gene Krupa's work in it, because I think he's probably the only man that would have that kind of quality to play drums like that...I have such a great respect for people that do those things with that kind of consistency, and that kind of application of their feelings toward it.

BUTCH MILES (drummer)

notes to Butch
Miles Salutes Gene
Krupa
(Famous Door),
1982

Gene was my first major influence way back when I was just beginning to play the set. I bought every Krupa record I could lay my hands on and then went searching for more...I stole every lick that Gene had and then invented some that I thought he used that I hadn't heard. I saw his movies and then, finally, the man in person...When Gene Krupa took a solo, you know it was a KRUPA solo. Nobody else sounded like him... Besides bringing the drummer to the forefront of the band and making him a high-priced musician, he was probably the nicest man who ever lived.

PEE WEE RUSSELL (clarinet)

notes to **Jazz at the
New School**
(Chiaroscuro), 1971

You play with Gene, you've got to play better. He insists.

NAT HENTOFF (author)

notes to **Krupa
Rocks**
(Verve), 1957

Whatever he does, the presence of strong emotion can always be felt in Krupa. He never coasts. He digs communicating because he has a lot of himself to give.

DAN MORGENSTERN (writer/editor/director Rutger's Institute of Jazz Studies)

Upon Krupa's in-
duction to the **down
beat Hall of Fame,**
December 21, 1972

A symbol of the swing era, and the man who put the jazz drum as solo instrument on the map.

LEONARD FEATHER (author/critic/composer/musician)

New Edition of the Encyclopedia of Jazz, Horizon, 1960

Gene Krupa was the first drummer in jazz history to attain a position of global renown, the most famous drummer in the history of jazz, the worldwide symbol of jazz percussion. His steady, relentless beat and ever-improving technique made him a vital figure in the years of Goodman's triumphs; his tremendous showmanship earned him renewed success as a leader in his own right.

GERRY MULLIGAN (saxophonist/bandleader), as told to Nat Hentoff

from *Jazz Is,* Ridge Press/Random House, 1976

While Mulligan was with Gene Krupa, the band had been working and travelling frenetically, and its playing in Mulligan's opinion had become shoddy. One night, at the end of a set, Mulligan rose and, in plain hearing of the audience, upbraided the band in general and then Krupa in particular for his inability or unwillingness to set higher standards. "I told them all to go to hell," Mulligan recalls. At a meeting of the band the next day, Krupa lit into the band first, and then into Mulligan for inexcusable behavior in public. Krupa proceeded to fire Mulligan, but he did not hold a grudge against his former employee. *I had to admire that guy,* Krupa said a few years later. *You get too much obsequiousness in this business. There was no obsequiousness in him, which I dug.*

LOUIS BELLSON (drummer/bandleader/arranger/composer)

interview with the author

Gene had a real part in influencing Buddy Rich and myself. We both respected Gene throughout many, many years, because I think he was the first guy who really brought the drums to the foreground. He made everybody aware of the fact that the drums were not only an instrument that supplied rhythm, but he also became a solo showcase in the band. So Gene is really responsible for that. We have to respect him and know that he did that.

ROY ELDRIDGE (trumpet)

**down beat
Magazine,**
May 18, 1951

One thing you can be sure of, as long as I'm in America, I'll never work with a white band again. It goes all the way back to when I joined Gene Krupa's band. Until that time no colored musician had worked with a white band except as a separate attraction, like Teddy and Lionel with Benny Goodman.

That was how I worked with Gene at first; I wasn't treated as a full member of the band. But very soon I started sharing Shorty Sherock's book, and when he left the band, I took over. It killed me to be accepted as a regular member of the band. But I knew I'd have to be awful cool; I knew all eyes were on me to see if I'd make time or do something wrong.

All the guys in the band were nice, and Gene was especially wonderful. That was at the Pennsylvania Hotel. Then we headed West for some one- nighters, winding up in California. That was when the trouble began.

We arrived in town and the rest of the band checks in. I can't get into their hotel, so I keep my bags and start riding around looking for another place, where someone's supposed to have made a reservation for me. I get there and move all my bags in. Naturally, since we're going to be out on the coast several months, I have a heavy load, at least a dozen pieces of baggage.

Then the clerk, when he sees that I'm the Mr. Eldridge the reservation was made for, suddenly discovers that one of their regular tenants just arrived and took the last available room. I lug that baggage back into the street and start looking around again.

By the time that kind of thing has happened night after night, it begins to work on my mind; I can't think right, can't play right. When we finally got to the Palladium in Hollywood, I had to watch who I could sit at the tables with. If they were movie stars who wanted me to come over, that was all right; if they were just the jitterbugs, no dice. And all the time the bouncer with his eye on me, just watching for a chance.

On top of that, I had to live way out in Los Angeles, while the rest of the guys stayed in Hollywood. It was a lonely life; I'd never been that far away from home before, and I didn't know anybody. I got to brooding.

Then it happened. One night the tension got so bad I flipped. I could feel it right up to my neck while I was playing *Rockin Chair*, I started trembling, ran off the stand and threw up. They carried me to doctor's. I had 105 degree fever; my nerves were shot.

When I went back a few nights later I heard that people were asking for their money back because they couldn't hear *Let Me Off Uptown*. This time they let me sit at the bar.

...Man, when you're on the stand, you're great, but as soon as you come off, you're nothing. It's not worth the glory, not worth the money, not worth anything. Never again!

(Author's note: Things had apparently improved a bit by 1949 — at least "mixed bands" had become more common — and Eldridge rejoined the Krupa crew in February of that year, leaving about nine months later to join the Jazz At The Philharmonic tour.)

Gene Krupa

INTERVIEWS:

- TEDDY WILSON
- CHARLIE VENTURA
- MARTY NAPOLEON
- JOHN BUNCH
- EDDIE WASSERMAN
- CARMEN LEGGIO
- BENNY GOODMAN

CHAPTER SIXTEEN

INTERVIEWS

TEDDY WILSON

Historically, pianist Teddy Wilson represents the keyboard link between Earl Hines and Bud Powell. He initially came to international attention via a John Hammond-produced recording session in 1933 led by Benny Carter. What cemented his fame, however, came as a result of joining the Benny Goodman fold in July of 1935, in what became the Benny Goodman Trio, and later, with the addition of Lionel Hampton on vibraphone, The BG Quartet. In the process, Wilson also became the first black man to perform regularly with a white orchestra (although it must be noted that Wilson did not play with the orchestra itself, he was featured only within the Trio and Quartet a few times per evening). After leaving Goodman in 1939, Wilson led a wonderful but short-lived big band, travelled with a sextet and later mostly trios throughout the fifties and sixties, and served on the staff of radio station WNEW in New York. Wilson's association with Krupa resumed in the early fifties, via the aborted Goodman reunion tour of 1953, the filming of *The Benny Goodman Story* in 1956, and later BG Quartet reunions right up until 1973 in what was Gene Krupa's last personal appearance. Wilson continued to play regularly and superbly in duo and trio formats until his death in 1986.

Interview

I did most of my early playing in New York with Gene
Krupa. I was with him for three solid years with Benny
Goodman from 1935 to 1938. Then I had made recordings
with him in studio sessions before Benny had the band, as
far back as 1934 or 1935. But practically every night for
three years, after Benny organized the band—in the Trio
and Quartet—I played with Gene. I played with him more
than any other drummer. Him and Cozy Cole in those
days, too, with the Willie Bryant and Benny Carter band.
I also did the last engagements Gene ever did at Saratoga
and in Chicago. Goodman got the original Quartet
together, and Chicago was in August, 1973, I think. I was
booked with him in Indianapolis shortly after that and
Gene couldn't make it. They got a local drummer.

Gene refined his style over all those years in his own
way. He never changed his style to what you'd call modern.
He never just started copying Max Roach or any of those
drummers that came up in the be-bop movement. He sort
of just refined and modernized what he did himself. The
Gene Krupa style never changed. It was so good from the
beginning that all he had to do was refine it and make little
changes in what was his normal growth and development.
But what a lot of people call modernizing is really a very
bad thing. It means you're throwing out your roots and
jumping over with a new wave, like drummers who would
jump over and start imitating Max Roach or Kenny Clarke,
or drummers who have come up since like Tony Williams
or Billy Higgins. The imitators throw out their own natural
way of playing drums and try to play **their** way which is only
natural for **them.** Just to be called modern. Well, you ruin
your music, I think.

Gene never did that, but Gene did get better right up
until the end. Whatever modernization was in there was
stuff he added that fitted what he had been doing, and the
knowledge of drumming that he had been resting on all
his life. He added no jarring note that conflicted with what
he had already been doing. That's the way all great artists
develop. You never shift your roots to the new wave or the
new fad, because if you do, you're lost. You become an
imitator.

I never had a drummer who could play as close to what I do as Gene Krupa. He played **exactly** the style of drums that went behind my piano and he knew how to do it. The best drumming I ever had — and the most comfortable drumming where the drums fitted by style — was from Gene Krupa more than any other drummer. Cozy Cole might be in that category, too, though Cozy played differently from Gene and I was a little closer to what Gene was doing.

We still have to listen to Gene Krupa, because Gene Krupa was using values that a lot of drummers today don't even know. A lot of drummers don't have any conception of how to use **the drums.** Some of today's drummers can play as good on a pad as they do on a $10,000 drum set. See, Gene had a **feeling** for the tone of every one of his drums, his snare, his bass drum and **each cymbal.** He was sensitive to the sound of each piece of his equipment and he made that sound a part of his work. Some drummers today would sound as good on a coffee table as they're ever going to sound.

There are other values they know nothing about, like the tone of each drum, making the drum speak with **meaning,** and making every stroke say something rather than a rattling kind of playing that most modern drummers do. When some of these modern guys get going, it sounds like a battlefield. You hear the machine guns, the small arms and the cannon. The old drummers, too, had an advantage over the younger drummer. They had to play behind acts, all sorts of musicians, dancers and people who do other things in show business. They knew how to fit the drums in behind other things than a trumpet or saxophone. Gene never played the same behind a piano that he did behind a saxophone. And then he didn't play the same behind every saxophone player! He played behind whatever was going at the moment. Gene would do on the drums what was most appropriate. Some younger drummers will play the same behind a piano as they do behind a trombone. You have to make the drums **meaningful,** not rattling. Otherwise, you can hook up one of those mechanical gadgets. The new ones will do anything! They can rattle as good as any drummer.

Gene Krupa was one of the nicest men I ever met in my whole life. I never saw Gene in a bad mood. I always had a happy association with him. He was one of my very favorite people and one of the finest men I ever knew. I could understand him in some sort of a psychological way and he could understand me.

CHARLIE VENTURA

The musician most closely associated with Gene Krupa over the years was saxophonist Charlie Ventura, who served tenures as featured soloist with the First Band from 1942-43, the Second Band from 1944-46, the Gene Krupa Jazz Trio within the second band, the revived Gene Krupa Jazz Trio of 1952, The Great New Quartet of 1962-64, and reunions with Gene in Philadelphia and New York in the early seventies. The Krupa Trio renditions of *Dark Eyes, Body and Soul* and *Stompin' At the Savoy* had long constituted the most requested items in the Ventura repertoire. Ventura later became a star in his own right with his "Bop for the People" group of the late forties, subsequent large following as a Las Vegas attraction, and appearances on the many Jackie Gleason "Mood Music" albums.

Ventura won the following awards: Number One tenor saxophonist, **down beat Magazine,** 1945; New Star on tenor saxophone, **Esquire Magazine,** 1946; Number One small group, **down beat Magazine,** 1948-49; Number One small group, **Metronome Magazine,** 1949; Number One tenor saxophonist (tied with Stan Getz), first **Playboy Jazz Poll,** 1957.

Ventura has made recent appearances at the Golden Nugget in Atlantic City area festivals and a brief European sojourn. He resides today in Atlantic City and due to illness is no longer playing. The following represents a relatively rare Ventura interview and sheds new light on the formation and development of the legendary Jazz Trio.

Interview

I was working at the Philadelphia Navy Yard in 1942 and got a call from Gene's manager. Roy Eldridge and I used to jam at places in Philly when he was in town, you know, and I think he recommended me. I turned it down first, but then the manager called again and I took it. This was in August 1942, in Hartford, Connecticut at the State Theater. I was making $85 a week. I didn't have any solos at the start, but I did one later and Gene liked it. That's how I became one of the featured soloists.

I think the Trio first happened when we were playing an engagement at the Hotel Sherman in Chicago, back in 1944. That's when Gene had the strings in the big band. You know, he was with Tommy Dorsey and he built his band like Dorsey's by adding nine strings, a vocal group and stuff like that. In the meantime, Gene approached me and Teddy Napoleon about making a trio, in that his background with Benny Goodman and the Benny Goodman Trio with Benny, Teddy Wilson and Gene was such an outstanding feature. Gene figures, "Can we do something like that?" He wanted to add the Jazz Trio as an addition to the shows he was doing.

He says to me, *Think of a few things and we'll try to blend it together.* At the moment, I was approached with no bass player, so what d'ya do? So, we had a few rehearsals, and the first thing we did was that *Dark Eyes* thing, and *Body and Soul* (March 8, 1945), and then a number of other things. We had to create some kind of feeling that there wasn't a bass missing. But once you hear a few things, you overlook the bass part. That was the inauguration of the Trio. We kept that as a feature. I enjoyed it very much. It was great!

I made most of the arrangements, like on *Fine's Idea*, which is based on the chords of *Blue Lou*. With the guys on 52nd Street like Parker and Gillespie, they would take tunes like *Indiana* and those kinds of tunes and use the chords then make up a new melody line. I figured that on the chord structure of *Blue Lou* I'd get a new line. In the forties a lot of the players used the chord changes to standard songs of that time.

During the time I had my club in New Jersey, The Open House, I sounded Gene. He was at home in Yonkers after his big band broke up. This was about 1952. I set up a deal with him and said we should re-do the Trio. I got Teddy Napoleon and Gene at my club for an indefinite stay. Joe Glaser, the booking agent from ABC (Associated Booking Corporation), he came down and he offered us this thing in Japan and Hawaii. That's how we got off the ground there.

We had an engagement at the Officer's Club in Hawaii for about three weeks and then another supper club. And while we were there we had notice that we were going to go to Japan, and we had to take all our shots.

(Ventura's comments in **down beat Magazine,** June 18, 1952: The experience was just too much. There was nothing the people wouldn't do for us. And they'd wait for hours just to get an autograph or take your picture or shake your hand. We'd get off the stand and waiting for us in the dressing room would be three little baskets of cold towels, three big bottles of beer, three stacks of sandwiches — everything in threes. Lines of people would file in with gifts for us — we still haven't had the time to open most of them. The Japanese musically? They're still at the stage of copying, rather than creating, but they sure can swing.)

In 1962, I rejoined Gene, when he had John Bunch on piano and Knobby Totah on bass. Then, we went to Japan again in 1964. In that band, when we had a rehearsal, we would all sit down, and come up with tunes and put a line to them. But with the addition of a bass player, Knobby Totah, naturally it was a different feel. And Gene was more modern. But we still did the things that Gene was noted for like *Stompin'*, *Sing, Sing, Sing, Big Noise from Winnetka, Dark Eyes, Body and Soul,* and all those things. It was a great band. Oh, I enjoyed that. We did a great album on Verve, too, **Great New Quartet.**

MARTY NAPOLEON

Pianist Marty Napoleon is the brother of the late Theodore George ("Teddy") Napoleon, pianist who logged more time with Gene Krupa than anyone else (1944-1958), including the Second Band, the Jazz Trios with Eddie Shu and Charlie Ventura, and some of the later Quartets with Shu and all-star combinations. As Krupa told Nat Hentoff in 1958 upon Napoleon's departure, *He plays with so much heart and verve. Those qualities are in his playing all the time. I sure hated to lose him, but he decided he'd been on the road too long. He had an 18-year-old daughter who hardly recognized him.*

Though Marty Napoleon's recognition has come as a result of his road time with the Louis Armstrong All-Stars, he actually replaced brother Teddy for a time in the Second Band of 1946, and worked some of Gene's last dates with Eddie Shu and bassist Milt Hinton in and around New York, including the Newport-in-New York/Singer Bowl Concert where Gene was honored by hundreds of drummers. Marty Napoleon's and Gene Krupa's careers ran parallel in other ways, too, in that both worked extensively with Charlie Ventura from the forties through the seventies.

Today, Marty Napoleon is more active than ever, leading his own groups in New York City, appearing in all-star combinations stateside and overseas with Armstrong Tribute groups, and more recently performing at the New Orleans World's Fair with none other than Grammy winner Wynton Marsalis. Napoleon is also working on his own memoirs, concerning his life on the road with Louis Armstrong.

Interview

I was working Child's Paramount Restaurant in Manhattan on Times Square. Gene Krupa was working at a place called the 400 Club which was on Fifth Avenue just off 42nd Street. One night I finished work and I went to see Teddy with the band. So I walked in. Gene's manager's name at the time was the drummer Joe Dale, and he said, "Want to sit in?" I said, "Gee, I'd love to." You know, I got nervous. So I sat in and played a set with the band, and then when I got off the bandstand Joe came over to me and said, "Do you know your brother Teddy's leaving?" I said, "No, I didn't." He said "Well, he gave his notice, and Gene likes the way you play. Would you like to go with the band?"

I was flabbergasted, first of all, because Teddy hadn't told me anything about it, and secondly because I just went in to see my brother play with the band and before I knew it...I went home I told my wife, "I got an offer to go with Gene's band!"

It's a funny thing. We did a lot of one-nighters in New Jersey, California, a whole bunch of things. I joined the band at the old Aquarium Restaurant in New York on

Seventh Avenue. They were going to California to make a picture which I didn't know about, so we went to California and made two pictures, a movie and a short. I was on the road with Gene and I got sick on the road. And then we were playing in Asbury Park and Gene came to me, and this is the God's honest truth, and he said, *You know, Marty, I love you, you're a great player, but Teddy would like to come back to the band.*

It was very nice, but I really wasn't thrilled about the band at that particular point. I don't know why. Maybe because I wasn't feeling well and wasn't enjoying the band like I should have, because we had great guys. We had Buddy Stewart, Don Fagerquist, Red Rodney, Charlie Kennedy, Gerry Mulligan. The band was just sensational, but I just wasn't feeling well. So when Gene told me Teddy wanted to come back in the band, I said, "Beautiful" and went back to New York.

Gene never played be-bop. The thing was that Gerry Mulligan was writing for the band. Gerry wrote *Disc Jockey Jump* and *How High the Moon.* And Ed Finckel wrote some things. These guys were young, and they were great writers and they were into the be-bop thing. So when Gene recorded these things and they became hits, what else could Gene do? I mean, he was definitely not a be-bop drummer. He had a very heavy foot. He was magnificent in the band, but if you took him out of that context and put him with, say, Red Rodney and a quartet, you'd say, you know, well, we don't want this. He was not a be-bop drummer. But he sounded great with the big band, because, let's face it, it was his band and he could do whatever he wanted to do and it came out just right.

Gene replacing Buddy Rich in The Big Four (Rich, Napoleon, Charlie Ventura and bassist Chubby Jackson comprised an amazing, but short- lived group for a time in 1950)? Buddy was giving us a hard time and Charlie was getting very unhappy. Buddy had already said he was going to leave to start another big band that Frank Sinatra was backing. Gene came in to see us at the Preview Lounge in Chicago. Charlie took Gene on the side and said, "Gene, Buddy's going to leave. Why don't you come with the group?" And you know what Gene said? He said, *Are you kidding? I could never do what you guys do!* We used to do a little thing called the *Evolution of Jazz.* Some of it was straight life and some of it was comedy, tongue-in-cheek style. We all used to impersonate all these vocalists and instrumentalists. We closed with Buddy doing Gene Krupa and he used to play it with his left hand! And it sounded just like Gene! And we did it when Gene was in the room! So later, when we all took Gene on the side and asked him to join, he said, *I could never do that.* We said, "Come on, Gene, what are you saying? You're Gene Krupa." He really, like, got panicky.

Just before Gene died, I did some dates with him, Eddie Shu and bassist Milt Hinton around the metropolitan area. He wasn't that busy, he was sort of semi-retired. This was just before his house had burnt down. He was in bad shape at that time. He had trouble with his ear, he had a slipped disc, and his wife left him with the kids. He was really depressed. The last time I saw him was when we worked the Singer Bowl for the Newport in New York Festival. We took a bus together from New York City out to the stadium. And he said, *You know, Marty, I got leukemia. Marty...what else, what else can happen to me? But thank God, it's one of these things where they can contain it, and I'm going to take some treatments for it.*

Gene was a very nice man. First of all, he was very religious...he always carried a Bible with him. He was always very gracious and very good to people.

JOHN BUNCH

Pianist John Bunch played with Gene Krupa's "Great New Quartets" from 1961 to 1965. Other than serving six years as Tony Bennett's musical director and pianist, Bunch has functioned primarily on a freelance basis, with everyone from Benny Goodman to Al Cohn.

In the past few years, Bunch has recorded a series of remarkable small group sides as a leader on independent labels like Famous Door, Concord Jazz and others.

Interview

I joined Gene around 1961, I think it was. I was playing with both he, Benny Goodman and the Al Cohn/Zoot Sims group. It always worked out real good, in that none of them had real full time bands. As a matter of fact, Gene was always very nice about that. He always let me take off to play with Benny. Eddie Wasserman was the tenor player when I joined. As a matter of fact, Eddie was the one who fixed it up to get me on the job.

Later on, Charlie Ventura became available. Now, none of this was a full time band, you know. In those days, Gene had a few weeks in one place and a few weeks in another place once in a while. No, there were no charts, no music written out for anything. I had to rehearse to learn the book.

Yeah, I got some backlash from the modern jazz fans back then, as to why I would be doing this job. In the beginning, I sort of had mixed feelings about Gene. To be very honest with you, I didn't appreciate his approach that much until after I joined the band. Then I realized what kind of person he was and how sincere he was. I used to think he was all showbiz. Then I began to realize he was very musical, very sincere, and that he wasn't putting anything on at all. All that smiling, and the hair flying and everything was really a very natural thing. He was very fortunate, though, to have that fantastic "look" about him. I'll give you an example. The first rehearsal I had with the band, he came up to my house. I had a set of drums and everything and a nice place to rehearse. That's when I found out that all that showbusiness "look" about him was totally sincere. He did the same movements and the same smiles in the rehearsal that he did on a job in public. That's when I realized he was sincere.

I did get to enjoy his playing very much. Sure, he had his faults like everyone else does, but I learned a lot from him about music and about piano playing, particularly about dynamics. Yes, playing-wise by then he had certainly slowed down.

Charlie Ventura? Yes, there were some problems, but he always played pretty good. Later on (about 1965), Charlie had some sickness and then an operation, so someone had to play. We got Carmen Leggio (who made a name for himself in Woody Herman's organizations), but never recorded with him. Carmen always sounded great, but there's no one like Charlie Ventura.

Around 1965 or so, Gene didn't have that much work, though we did get to Japan and Mexico City, where we were very well received. That's when I left the band.

EDDIE WASSERMAN

Multi-reedman Eddie Wasserman performed as a sideman in many of the big bands in the forties, before and after graduating from the Juilliard School of Music in 1948. He joined Krupa in 1957 and stayed for five years. Wasserman was the focal point — with his tenor sax, flute and clarinet — of what was one of Krupa's most modern-sounding and versatile groups. Today, Wasserman performs infrequently as a jazz soloist, as he's heavily involved in teaching — in the public school system and privately — in the Clinton, New Jersey area.

Interview

I played with a series of bands, like Benny Goodman, Artie Shaw and Stan Kenton, and got with Gene by way of reputation November of 1957. I had done some record dates with him in 1955 and 1956, but came in the Quartet permanently to replace a clarinet player, Gale Curtis, who came between Eddie Shu and myself. Gale didn't really fit in.

Some have said that I gave the group a more progressive sound, but actually (the late) Eddie (Shu) was more progressive than me. He's a very talented guy. He's a fantastic talent and a natural talent. I think he has perfect pitch. He's more like Charlie Parker in that sense than I am. But he does not play **the instruments** that well in terms of things like intonation. For what it's worth, I just think of music differently that he does. I think of music a little like Benny Goodman does. I'm not afraid to play the melody. Our pianist for a time, Ronnie Ball, did have something of a reputation as a modernist. He had been into studying with Lennie Tristano. But as you hear on our records, he was a very heavy rhythm player. In fact, Ronnie practiced with a metronome.

And Gene liked, like anybody, a heavy rhythm player. He didn't care if the notes were be-bop or not. Just so the time was there.

I used to get comments from all the musicians in New York like, "How can you play with this guy night after night?" I'd say, "Well, who would you rather play with night after night, Gene Krupa or Buddy Rich?" They got the message. Gene could play when he wanted to. He'd have to be sort of motivated. Sometimes, he'd just goof off. Not very often. But if someone would come into the room — like a pretty gal or a musician — then he'd play. All I can say is that when Ronnie Ball, bassist Jimmy Gannon and I all got together, we'd really **play**, always. We made some great records.

I was with Gene for five years and I never had any disagreements with him, and that's a long time to be playing jazz with someone night after night. About the only thing I can think of in terms of "words" that we ever had was in Chicago one night (probably at the London House). This is when he got married to that young gal, Pat Bowler. Gene was affected by it, you know what I mean? In a good way. He started calling rehearsals, and he never called any rehearsals. I guess he just wanted things to be first class for her. Well, we rehearsed something just that afternoon and we started to play it that night. Now, there was never any definite way to play a tune. It would sort of evolve. We'd play, we'd add to it, and it would sort of come into being. I think the tune was *Caravan*. Remember, the way to do anything was never set until later. Well, we came to the end of the tune and Gene said something to the effect of, *I'm going to have to start hollering for accuracy!* So I said, "Gene, are you going to start hollering at yourself?" And he looked at me and got mad. So, we went outside and he said something, and then he started to laugh. That was the extent of it.

While we were on the road we'd go out and play baseball in the summertime. Gene was always a big baseball fan. We'd go out, shag flies, get some exercise to work off the hangovers. That was about the only kind of "playing around" that Gene did on the road. There really wasn't much of it. Not from him. The only time I think he really did, for what it's worth, was when he had his heart attack and I think he must have figured he could go at any time. But I never saw it. Now, we were never that close socially. Oh, we got along fine and I was at his house and his office, but I normally just saw him on the job.

I contracted the band for the Krupa/Buddy Rich **Burnin Beat** album for Verve Records in 1962. No, there was no rivalry between them in the studio and nothing really interesting went on. Because Buddy Rich wasn't even there! Buddy dubbed his part over. I'm telling you! Nobody believes it! The spaces were there in the arrangements for Buddy's parts and Buddy came in later and recorded his parts over, after Gene had already done his with the band. Yeah! The drum battles on that record? Well, as far as I know, Buddy just wasn't there at all. He did that taped over later on by putting on earphones and playing his part.

(Author's note: Because of photographs taken in-studio by Charles Stewart of Krupa and Rich setting up their equipment, we must presume that at least one of the "drum duels" on that recording — *Duet* and/or *Evolution* — were recorded live, in-studio by Gene Krupa and Buddy Rich.)

CARMEN LEGGIO

Though tenor saxophonist Carmen Leggio was best known as a modern, Sonny Rollins-influenced tenor saxophonist with the great Woody Herman Herds of the early sixties, he was always a most flexible player, what with credentials ranging from tenures with Benny Goodman to Terry Gibbs to Maynard Ferguson. He was with Gene Krupa in what was one of Gene's final, regularly working groups, from 1964 to 1966. Today, Leggio resides in Tarrytown, New York, working on recording for and marketing on his own label.

Interview

Charlie Ventura got sick and had to have an operation and I took his place. I took his place in early 1964 and I was with Gene two years. I was working The Metropole a lot in those days and I guess I was heard, you know. That was when things were going strong at The Metropole, and Gene just came up and asked me if I would sub for Charlie. After that, Charlie had the operation so I stayed. Yeah, I was considered a pretty modern player in those days and still am. But when Gene was on, and he was wailing and feeling good, he had immaculate time and as far as I was concerned he was a master of dynamics. The most important thing was that he swung and he swung the hell out of that ride cymbal. He was a swinger, his time was immaculate, and I could play with him better than I could with a lot of other people, you know what I mean? Let's put it this way: when he was feeling good, Gene was on the nose, and I could play better with him that I could with a lot of modern drummers that really weren't into the time. Gene used every part of the drums, especially the bass drum.

I'll tell you the truth about learning the arrangements. When I subbed for Charlie Ventura, I had to come in blind, we rehearsed as we went along. Gene just kept talking to me on the bandstand. He gave me the list of tunes, told me what to play—though I knew most of them—and he just talked to me as we went along. Arrangements were just made on the bandstand.

Many times I got comments from the young, modern cats as to why I was doing this gig. But I enjoyed him as a person and I enjoyed him as a musician. Naturally, it was a show and we played all the old tunes, but I have the ability to not get stagnant. I look at music like there's no end to the variations. In my solos, I never really played the same thing twice. As far as the arrangements on things like *Dark Eyes* and *Sorrento*, those were set arrangements, but as far as my solos, I always variated. Gene **never** told me how to play.

I'll tell you the truth, as a human being, Gene was 100 percent, very spiritual. After we finished playing at the Metropole many times at 3:00 in the morning, I drove him to church. He'd go to church, say his prayers and then go to sleep. He was a very religious man. When we were on the road, I don't care where it was, on Sunday he'd say *Get off the highway and find me a church*. He was a good person. He treated me very well, and there was never any problem with money or taxes or anything. Everything was done right.

He was feeling good in those days, maybe slowing down a little, but what bothered him was that he adopted two kids and had gotten married again, and he just wanted to be at home as much as he could. That's what bothered him. So if we were in California and had a day off on a Sunday, he would fly home to see his wife and kids. He was bothered by the personal life. He was lonely, he lived like a hermit in the hotel rooms, you know. All that happened was, he'd go to the job at night, and then a lot of times so no one would recognize him, he'd go to the White Tower after the job to have a hamburger. Then he'd go to sleep, somebody would wake him up at 6:00 in the morning for an interview, then he'd come back to the room, have something sent up to the room or maybe go and have a little lunch out, maybe do another interview in the room for television. Most everytime, everything was sent up to his room, so his life was in the room. And so whenever we'd have a day off, I don't care where he was, he'd go home.

Even by then, Gene was still a top attraction wherever we went, especially when we went to South America. They **really** rolled out the red carpet for him. We did about 17 television shows down there and were treated very, very well. We also did the Dean Martin Show and the Mike Douglas Show, Al Hirt Show and some shows in Chicago. Around 1966, before we left for Vegas, I went to his house, we opened up his closet and looked through all his big band material. What we did was we drove out to Vegas, and they contracted a big band around the Quartet. That was probably the last big band that he every played with. We did *Let Me Off Uptown*, *Disc Jockey Jump*, *Lover*, and some others. The Quartet played first, then the big band. This was at the Tropicana. Gene sounded beautiful. He was really happy. Those charts were still good.

That's about when I left. I left because I just needed to get off the road. There was never any problem or dissension between us. He treated me like a son.

BENNY GOODMAN

Benny Goodman's history need not be recounted here. What is worth noting is that, as a result of this very brief and surprising conversation, it can accurately be stated—hopefully for the final time—that most of the stories heard about the late King's personality, or the lack of it, were true.

Interview

What more can I say about Gene Krupa? I think I've said everything I can say. It's all in the books and you have all my records. All I guess that I can say is that he was a wonderful human being. You know the story. He was in my band, of course, and left to run his own band which was rather successful. Yes, you know I played some concerts with him just before he died. Did he play any differently at the end than when he first joined by band? No, I wouldn't say so. He sounded, to me, pretty much the same. He was rather consistent. We had a great association over the years. When did you say he died? 1973? He died rather young, didn't he? What a shame.

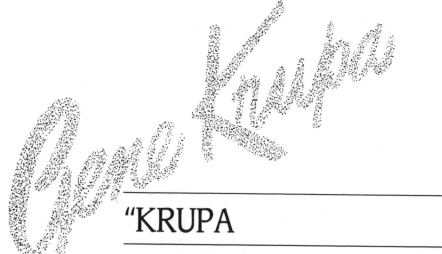

"KRUPA

AND THE

SYMPHONY"

CHAPTER SEVENTEEN

KRUPA AND THE SYMPHONY

Originally published
in **Esquire
Magazine**
February, 1947

To the uninitiated who know nothing of Gene Krupa and Leonard Bernstein other than, say, what they have seen on television, the two men would seem to have little in common except their unruly shocks of hair. Yet they share at least one trait that has strongly influenced both their professional lives: each has a deep love of the other's type of music. At home, Krupa, the frenetic and inspired swing drummer, listens almost exclusively to symphonic music — albums by Delius, Ravel, Milhaud, Stravinsky, Debussy. For his personal pleasure, Bernstein, the symphonic conductor and classical composer, listens to the recordings of such as Teddy Wilson, Bix Beiderbecke, Eddie Condon, Pee Wee Russell, Max Kaminsky and Gene Krupa.

My good friend Leonard Bernstein says that symphonic music, "serious" music written for performance by the full orchestra, has been influenced by jazz. The jazz influence is said by some critics to be especially apparent in Bernstein's own compositions.

I disagree. I have never heard anything genuinely and honestly derivative of jazz in any such music, even, maybe especially, in such works as Igor Stravinsky's "Ebony Suite" ("Concerto"), which Woody Herman, with his usual swing instrumentation, brilliantly performed in Carnegie Hall and several other places. I've never heard it in any of the "serious" pieces of George Gershwin, who, anybody will tell you, was preeminently "the American jazz composer."

But then, I've never heard it, as has John Hammond, in the works of Darius Milhaud, for all that during his American visit in the early thirties, Milhaud listened, entranced, to the unsurpassable jazz virtuosity at the hot piano of such great artists as Fats Waller, Earl Hines and Jimmy Johnson. I watched Maurice Ravel, at the old Sunset in Chicago, marvel at Jimmy Noone's transcendent clarinet. Jimmy could fly over a clarinet like no one before him or since—ask Benny Goodman—and it was undoubtedly Noone's technical virtuosity, not the music itself, which obsessed Maurice Ravel. For all his preoccupation with rhythm, I've never heard the least echo of that music, or any music like it, in his compositions.

Leonard Bernstein and others profess to hear traces, echoes, derivations of jazz in Frederick Delius, John Alden Carpenter, Manuel De Falla, Honegger, Prokofieff, even Shostakovich.

The influence of jazz has been found by someone or other, unnecessarily eager to make out a case for jazz that it doesn't need, anxious perhaps to endow it with reflected "respectability" so that he won't need to make excuses to himself and others for liking it, in the works of these composers. But, in my opinion, it isn't there.

Let's pay a little more attention to two of the composers mentioned earlier—Stravinsky and Gershwin. They are reputed to show the most jazz influence. The contention might well stand or fall with them.

Stravinsky did evince preoccupation with jazz music. He talked about it. He wrote a series of compositions with titles referring to "ragtime" but no evidence of that preoccupation appears in the actual music, honestly examined, honestly listened to. That preoccupation was purely verbal. Although apparently able to sense, to feel, the jazz tempo, he has been unable to express it. His tremendous musical vitality did not encompass the peculiar rhythmic, driving, let us say American quality which is the essence of jazz.

Nor is that essence to be found in that more pretentious work of George Gershwin. It exists in the blues feeling of some of his popular songs, particularly when played in the authentic jazz spirit by authentic jazz instrumentalists. But it does not exist in his "Concerto in F"—even if in some passages he did use derbies to mute the trumpets.

His "Rhapsody in Blue," which too often has been labeled The Jazz Symphony, is much more — as is Gershwin's serious work as a whole — in the tradition of Claude Debussy. I don't believe the opening of "L'Apres-midi d'une Faunce" is reminiscent of Noone's clarinet work.

Does this mean that I believe that jazz can never and will never form a part of the mainstream of America's and of the world's music? To say it can't is to say that America, out of itself, has nothing to contribute musically to the world. Jazz is the United States' own native, original musical idiom.

Jazz can be the basis of great music to be written by an American composer just as much as, say Czech folk tunes were the basis of the music of Smetana and Dvorak.

But jazz can only make its proper contribution to the whole of music; will only make that contribution when both the composition and performance of the music which is developing out of it are executed by musicians who are completely at home in the idiom. Music must be both conceived and performed, composed and played.

And jazz cannot be approached unsympathetically.

Too many "good," "pure" and "serious" musicians, and let's admit that, composing and playing in the idiom to which they are accustomed, are "good" musicians — approach the native American idiom, the jazz idiom, with intolerance, even with condescension. They stoop, but not to conquer. And so, they almost invariably make an unholy mess of their attempts. Then, of course, they sneer at jazz. They tell anyone who will listen that the stuff wasn't music in the first place, but naturally. However, the failure was with them, and all the name calling in the world cannot disguise that fact.

Are there in existence musicians who can compose and, equally important, play this music? A generation ago my answer would have had to be no. The traditional "great men" of jazz, Johnny Dodds and Frank Teschemacher on the clarinet, Joe Oliver, Louis Armstrong and others on the trumpet, Earl Hines and James P. Johnson, Jess Stacy and Fats Waller at the piano, Chick Webb and Baby Dodds at percussion, were not such, even if it is almost blasphemy to say so. It wasn't their fault. They were great musicians in spite of it. But they came up the hard way. All of them played for dough, played professionally, many while they were still in short pants. They never had the chance to get highly technical, classical training. And, essentially, they were performers, virtuosos, not creators. At most, they were improvisors. They achieved a certain measure of greatness in performance because they'd never been told that this or that was "impossible." They achieved, through very lack of classical training, effects which transcended themselves and their instruments. Don't misunderstand me. I'm not questioning their inherent musicianship. Louis Armstrong, "Satchmo," one of the greatest jazz trumpeters, could stand up in front of the New York Philharmonic and improvise a brilliant contrapuntal concerto flawless in color and tone against anything they might play.

But the great jazz masters didn't and don't have what musicians must have to achieve the kind of music we hope to achieve in America—musical discipline and a comprehensive musical background. They were locked within their limitations, and they were utterly unable to understand anything beyond the one segment of music which they "were," the music they sensed rather than knew. They could only play what they "felt" inside themselves. They were completely incapable of going beyond it. Consequently, the music they played, as "they" played it, was limited by their limitations.

Most jazzmen, at any rate a lot of them, were never at ease with musical notation. If they attempted to "learn" something musical, some passage, some effect, they sweated it out in rehearsal. Their music, and I must repeat again, as "they" played it, was caged in, locked in. It couldn't go much beyond its start. Within their own field, they showed genius, but the field was narrow and specialized.

But those limitations are not, I must emphasize again, inherent in jazz, natural to the idiom itself. Once the fetters are removed, America's own musical idiom is capable of limitless development.

Let me pass along a word, with great respect, to Mr. Stokowski and Mr. Koussevitzky and their august brethren:

"Gentlemen, if you should sometime in the future schedule for performance a work based on jazz, containing jazz passages, when such music is written, don't entrust its execution entirely to the regular members of your organizations. They are highly competent musicians — but this is not for them.

"The most skilled cordon bleu would look silly beside a Rhode Island cook at a shore dinner, or a ranch hand at a barbeque.

"American music, jazz music, must be played by men who were brought up to drink rye and coke in juke joints. A lifetime of blond beer in Munich or Torino Vermouth isn't quite the same thing.

"So, when you present American music, music growing out of jazz, make sure it is played by American musicians brought up in its tradition.

"There are such musicians, men who feel jazz and who are the musical equals otherwise of the regular members of your orchestras. They weren't a generation ago. But they are now.

"Try them.

"That's the only 'way,' Maestros, you will ever find out what American music has to offer you and to offer the world."

Some of the top men today, and a great many more of the musicians coming up, have the greatness of jazz's legendary figures. They were brought up in the idiom, they feel it, it's part of them and they are part of it, just as much as in the cases of Teschemacher and Dodds, Beiderbecke and the rest.

They have the same greatness, and even though it sounds somehow irreverent to write it down, they have a lot more. Sentiment aside, they have all the background, the knowledge, the education and training their predecessors lacked. In them, the jazz idiom, the jazz technique, the native music of America, enters into the mainstream of music. These musicians are part of jazz. They are also part of the world's musical tradition.

They are the ones who will write and play the new music, the American music that has its roots in and flows from jazz, flows from the trumpets of Bix Beiderbecke and Louis Armstrong and the piano fingers of James P. Johnson, from Eddie Condon's guitar and from Pee Wee Russell's clarinet.

Everyone knows that Bix Beiderbecke was among the jazz immortals as a trumpet player. But not everyone knows that, were it not for his untimely death, he might today be producing the sort of music I've been talking about. He seemed to be approaching it in "In a Mist," "Flashes,"

"Candelights," and "In the Dark," which compositions constitute his piano suite. Eastwood Lane was so impressed by Bix's ideas on composition that he sent for Bix, who spent some time working with Lane. But death silenced Bix's trumpet, and prevented his expressing to the world the music which may have been within him.

What will the American music developed out of the jazz idiom be like? I don't pretend to know what Bix's answer might have been, had he lived. But I have, for what it's worth, an answer of my own.

Top priority on my time is now being given to a musical experiment, an experiment in composition, the result of which I hope you'll hear some time soon.

It will be a composition, in concerto form, written for a swing band, with the usual brass, rhythm and reed sections, and for a 70-man symphony orchestra. The melodic contrapuntal line, the hot solos and jazz rhythms, will be played by musicians who know how to play them. The broad masses of harmony, the swelling legatos, will be played by musicians, the symphony musicians, who know how to play them. In its present outlined form my tentative concerto for "swing band and symphony" has three movements. First is a moderate tempo blues. Second is the drag, the tragic slow blues. And last is a frenzied, wild boogie. It will take, as I plan it now, about 25 minutes to play.

Even if my particular experiment is not too successful, it will represent what I think will be the coming American music. And it is the kind of music I want to hear. I want to hear a jazz solo weaving its intricate, dynamic melodic line across the powerful harmonies of a full symphony orchestra. I want to hear a quartette or trio of horns improvising against the background of 50 violins.

That's when the symphony will meet jazz as far as I am concerned.

LEONARD BERSTEIN'S REPLY

(Author's note: Then, as now, the Maestro leaned toward verbosity. The following, therefore, is something of an abridged version of his comments.)

I wholeheartedly submit the thesis that serious music in America would today have a different complexion and direction were it not for the profound influence upon it of jazz...

While most of us recall that wild post war era (World War I) with mixed feelings, the reflection of that decade in American music was brilliantly clear. There was a necessity to be original, to be chic, to be American. But now no Dvorak was needed to promulgate a movement. Something new had been added. Jazz had come to stay...

The really remarkable thing about jazz for the serious composer was that it solved simultaneously the two problems of being original and being American. For here at last was a musical material which was everybody's bread and butter. No real American could fail to understand a symphonic work which sounded like jazz. Now everyone would feel at home...

The man who gave this post war movement life, controversy and real genius was George Gershwin. His aim, in contradistinction to that of the "serious" composers, was to make of the materials of jazz, with which he was so intimate, a sort of symphonization in the tradition of the European masters, rather than to paste jazz onto already crystalized personal styles and forms, as did Stravinsky and Ravel. Gershwin approached this great merger from the left, so to speak, from the realm of wah-wah mutes and ga-ga chorus girls.

So it is with our *Rhapsody in Blue*, a succession of magnificent and inspired tunes connected in a haphazard way by Lisztian cadenzas, Tchaikovskian sequences, and Debussyan ramblings. And it stands today as a real monument to the terrific, but oh so imperfect, twenties...

(Regarding the serious music of the thirties)...something "inner" in jazz has entered our serious music. In every case it is not the superficial "jazziness" that should be sought, but a more profound influence: the cross relations in melodic writing, the peculiarly American sentimentality of harmonization, the intense freedom of the counterpoint, the glorious instrumental color that derives particularly from Negro wind-playing...

I recommend careful listening to and study of the works of Copland, Harris, Sessions, Schuman, and Barber, to name only a few...for analyses and diagnoses notwithstanding, the great synthesis goes irrevocably on.

THE
BEAT OF
THE DRUM

CHAPTER EIGHTEEN

THE BEAT OF THE DRUM

Though the following piece appeared under Gene Krupa's byline in a somewhat hysterically-written "fanzine" of the swing era — **Band Leaders**/July, 1945 — it does offer some valuable insights on Krupa's thoughts about African drumming and its influence on American jazz. In that **Band Leaders** was a "mass-market" publication and not a music or trade journal, some of the piece is, to say the least, rudimentary. Those sections have been omitted from the following material.

by GENE KRUPA

...I have been intensely interested in the native drummers of Africa for many years, and one of the most interesting experiences I've had was while playing with some genuine native African drummers.

This happened during the last World's Fair held in New York. I was playing there with my band at the time, and used to listen to the native drummers who were part of the sideshow operated by Frank "Bring 'em Back Alive" Buck.

In order to become better acquainted with their art, I attempted to become friendly with them, but, at first, found it very hard to gain their confidence.

Later on, when they realized my intentions were serious, they taught me many of their beats, and even sat in with the band.

A curious thing about native music, I discovered, is that while much of it follows the four-four pattern of modern dance music, the natives seem to count it in multiples of three.

My interest in this type of drumming was first seriously aroused when I obtained some records of native drumming which had been made by the Ross-Denis (sic) expedition.

I played these records over and over, and realized what wonderful rhythmic excitement stemmed from the Dark Continent.

That this should be, is not so strange. All of Africa is full of rhythm. Have you ever watched a walking elephant swaying slowly from side to side, in perfect rhythm, like a giant metronome?

I don't think it is going too far to assume that the African native, himself, has noticed this, and made it the basis of one of his beats. For I believe that many of his rhythms have been adapted from jungle noises and other sounds he hears.

The sounds of civilization, for example.

I know this sounds illogical, but in the records of which I spoke, is a rhythmic beat which sounds strangely reminiscent of the gasoline age.

It is a quick pattering rhythmic pattern, which to me, sounds like nothing so much as the putt-putt of a motor boat chugging up a jungle- sealed river on a foggy night.

And another of the beats surely must be derived from a culture other than Africa's own. For it sounds like the beat of a regimental drummer of an English army.

I don't mean to give the impression, of course, that all African drumming can be translated into modern terms, for it cannot. In adapting it for my own purposes I have to take liberties with it.

But I can and do base rhythms I use on basic African beats.

A good example of this is our record of "Blue Rhythm Fantasy," in which I improvise against three distinct rhythm patterns which are integrated into a major rhythmic theme, adapted from Bahutu chants and dances.

This sort of thing is typical of Afroic drumming. Native drummers, in fact, seldom play alone, but rather in groups, with specific parts assigned to each individual.

They also are able to obtain tonal effects of varying pitch by depressing the drum head with their hands, and by reason of the fact that many drums are tuned (in minor thirds) like modern instruments.

Snare drums seem to be unknown to native drummers, and they do not play with sticks as we do, but rather with mallets, or with their hands...

Gene Krupa

DEATH

AND

TRIBUTES

CHAPTER NINETEEN

DEATH AND TRIBUTES

Gene Krupa died October 16, 1973, about 9:30 a.m. at his Yonkers, New York, home. The official cause of death was listed as heart failure, though it had been widely known that Krupa was suffering from leukemia, as well as emphysema, heart problems and other ailments.

Reverend Joseph Marshall presided over a requiem mass at St. Denis Roman Catholic Church in Yonkers on October 18. The day before, there was a wake at Maloney's Funeral Home in Yonkers. Those in attendance included Benny Goodman, Buddy Rich, Helen Ward, Mel Lewis, Teo Macero, Frank Ipolito, Sam Ulano, Tommy Benford, Eddie Shu, John Bunch, Lenny Hambro and Nabil "Knobby" Totah.

After the requiem on the 18th, Krupa's body was taken to Chicago, where another wake was held at the Sodowski Funeral Home. On October 20, another mass was held at Immaculate Conception Church. Gene Krupa was buried on October 20 at Holy Cross Cemetery in Calumet City, Illinois.

Shortly after Krupa's death, his long-time associate, Frank Belinno, announced the establishment of The Gene Krupa Memorial Fund for Retarded Children, which operated out of Yonkers.

In addition to the Krupa tributes aired on all three major television networks' evening news slots on the evening of his death, a Gene Krupa Memorial Concert was held early in 1974 at New York City's Felt Forum. Featured at the show were a Krupa alumni band, Anita O'Day, Roy Eldridge, Urbie Green, Johnny Mince, Pee Wee Irwin, Milt Hinton, Lionel Hampton, Teddy Wilson, Buddy Rich, Dizzy Gillespie, Charlie Ventura, Ruby Braff, George Barnes, Bobby Hackett, Buddy Miles, Louis Bellson, Roy Haynes, Mickey Sheen, Roy Burns. Ed Sullivan was the M.C. Proceeds from the show went to The Retarded Children's Foundation.

In the years following Krupa's death, there had been intermittent talk about the formation of a Krupa "ghost" band, ala Glenn Miller, Tommy Dorsey, etc. Fronting and/or starring in the band would be either Roy Eldridge, Charlie Ventura and Anita O'Day. Apparently, that particular idea never progressed beyond the preliminary, "talking" stage, though O'Day has done some New York dates with a scaled-down "Krupa Tribute" outfit. Drummer Barrett Deems briefly fronted a "Krupa Tribute" band, and a west coast-based concert production company specializing in nostalgia packages put together what was called "The Gene Krupa Orchestra" for a limited 1986 tour. The drummer was Brent Brace, and Mel Tormé did a few concerts with the band.

The Krupa image is still very much with us, however, by way of an almost constant flow of reissued recordings and never-before-issued airchecks on LP and CD, home videos (*The Gene Krupa Story* was released in 1988), discographies and books. Ernst Ronowski, a GK-devotee based in West Germany, published a superlative two-volume bio-discography. Stateside, Charles Garrod and Bill Korst put out a thinner, but still informative double set.

APPENDIX

GENE KRUPA CHRONOLOGY

1909 – Born Eugene Bertram Krupa, Chicago, Illinois, January 15.

1920 – Brother Pete buys Gene first drum set.

1921 – Krupa joins "kid band," The Frivolians.

1924-1925 – Enrolled at St. Joseph's College in Indiana, a preparatory seminary.

1926-1927 – Works with commercial bands around Chicago, including Seattle Harmony Kings, Hoosier Bell Hops, Joe Kayser, Benson Orchestra of Chicago, Leo Shukin, girl bass player Thelma Terry. **December 9, 1927:** first recording on Okeh label with McKenzie-Condon Chicagoans, the first known recording to include the use of a bass drum.

1928 – Krupa moves to New York, early that year. **July:** first recording date with Red Nichols, then a sideman with Miff Mole. **Late July:** Recording of two sides for English Pathé label with Eddie Condon's Quartet. **September:** Recording of two sides on Vocalion label with Wingy Manone's Club Royale Orchestra. **December:** Recording of two sides for Okeh with Bud Freeman and Red McKenzie. **Late December:** Joins Red Nichols Orchestra in New York.

1929 – **September and December:** Recording with Eddie Condon and Fats Waller for Victor. Victor finds them so wild that they're issued on Victor's "race" label. **Beginning in August:** Krupa takes part in the beginning of 25 Red Nichols' recording dates, extending to June, 1931.

1930 – **May:** Recording for Victor under Hoagy Carmichael's leadership includes Bix Beiderbecke, Bubber Miley, Tommy and Jimmy Dorsey, Benny Goodman, Harry Goodman, Bud Freeman, Joe Venuti, Eddie Lang, Irv Brodsky, **July:** Recording for Victor under Beiderbecke's leadership.

1931-1934 — Leaves Nichols, 1931. Plays with Russ Columbo, **1932,** later Irving Aaronson's Commanders and Mal Hallett. **1933:** Marries Ethel Maguire. **October, 1933:** Recording for Columbia under Benny Goodman's leadership. **November/December 1933:** Two more sessions with Goodman, a band which included singer Billie Holiday. **February, 1934:** More recording with Goodman.

1935 — **April 4:** Krupa, at John Hammond's urging, leaves the Buddy Rogers band at the College Inn in Chicago to join the Benny Goodman band, at a reported salary of $87.50 per week (some sources, however, insist Krupa joined Goodman December 22, 1934). **Summer:** Beginning of the Benny Goodman Trio, featuring Krupa, Goodman and Teddy Wilson. **July 13:** First recording of the Benny Goodman Trio. **Late summer:** First Goodman triumph at Palomar Ballroom in Los Angeles.

1936 — Vibraphonist Lionel Hampton joins the Trio, to form the Benny Goodman Quartet. Hamp sometimes doubles on drums within the big band.

1937 — **March:** Wild, east coast triumph for Goodman at New York City's Paramount Theater.

1938 — **January 16:** The premier of jazz at New York's Carnegie Hall. **March:** Krupa leaves Goodman after a blowup at Phildelphia's Earle Theater. **April 16:** Krupa opens with his own band at Atlantic City's Steel Pier. **Latter 1938:** First film appearance as actor/bandleader, second billed to Bob Hope, in *Some Like it Hot*.

1941 — Divorce from wife Ethel. **March:** Vocalist Anita O'Day joins band. **April:** Trumpeter Roy Eldridge joins band.

1942 — Charlie Ventura joins band.

1943 — **April:** First recordings, or V-Discs, of Gene Krupa Trio with Buddy DeFranco/Dodo Marmorosa. **Early Summer:** Krupa arrested for possession of marijuana and contributing to the delinquency of a minor in San Francisco. Krupa pleads guilty to possession charge, not guilty to delinquency charge. Serves 84 days of a 90-day sentence. Eighteen months later, Krupa cleared of all charges. Roy Eldridge struggles to keep Krupa band together, but it breaks up. **September:** Krupa rejoins Benny Goodman and appears at New Yorker Hotel. **December:** Krupa joins Tommy Dorsey Orchestra in unbilled appearance at Paramount Theater, where he receives a tremendous ovation.

1944 — **June 11:** Leaves Tommy Dorsey to reform own orchestra. **June 21:** A nine-piece string section under Paul Nero's direction begins rehearsals. **June 26:** The full band, "The Band that Swings with

Strings," is assembled. **July 4:** First engagement in Hartford, Connecticut. **Latter 1944:** Remarries Ethel.

1945 — January: Krupa appears at Norman Granz' first recorded Jazz At The Philharmonic concert. **March 8:** First commercial recordings of The Gene Krupa Jazz Trio featuring saxophonist Charlie Ventura and Teddy Napoleon results in *Dark Eyes* and *Body and Soul.* **Circa June:** String section dropped. **July 7:** Vocalist Anita O'Day rejoins band.

1946 — January: Arranger/saxophonist Gerry Mulligan joins band, on alto sax, as does bop trumpeter Red Rodney. Ventura departs that summer and Buddy Wise becomes featured tenor until 1950.

1947 — Rodney and Mulligan depart.

1949 — February: Roy Eldridge rejoins. **Circa October:** Eldridge departs.

1950 — Switches to RCA label after 12 years on Columbia. **December:** Krupa breaks up big band.

1951 — February: Krupa reforms smaller version of big band (12 pieces plus two vocalists). Breaks up big band for good at year's end. Begins studies with New York Philharmonic tympanist Saul Goodman.

1952 — January: Reforms Gene Krupa Jazz Trio with Ventura and Napoleon, appearing at Jazz At The Philharmonic, nightclubs. **April:** Trio travels to Japan. **June:** Ventura departs. **July:** Tours Sweden with Flip Phillips taking over saxophone chair. **October:** Saxist Willie Smith and pianist Hank Jones comprise the Trio at JATP Carnegie Hall Concert. First recorded drum battle with Buddy Rich at that same show.

1953 — Spring: Joins Benny Goodman-Louis Armstrong tour, takes over leadership of Goodman band upon Goodman's departure. **May:** Begins recording, while not on JATP shows, with all-star pick-up groups for Norman Granz, which include Charlie Shavers, Ben Webster, Teddy Wilson, Lockjaw Davis. **December:** Multi-instrumentalist Eddie Shu joins Krupa and Napoleon as permanent Trio member.

1954 — March: Krupa opens drum school with Cozy Cole in New York in March. **October:** 11-show Australian tour with Shu and Napoleon. **December:** English bassist John Drew joins, making the Trio a Quartet. Takes part in filming of *The Glenn Miller Story.*

1955 — July: Krupa takes part in filming "Benny Goodman Story," and reunion recording with Teddy Wilson and Lionel Hampton. Pianist Bobby Scott replaces Teddy Napoleon in Jazz Quartet, bassist Whitey Mitchell replaces John Drew from May to November. **November 1:** First in-studio drum duel with Buddy Rich backed by JATP All-Stars.

1956 – Wife Ethel dies. Pianist Dave McKenna replaces Scott. **February:** First Gene Krupa Orchestra "reunion recording" for Norman Granz, featuring Roy Eldridge and Anita O'Day on Krupa big band hits.

1957 – **October:** Eddie Wasserman replaces Eddie Shu in Jazz Quartet.

1958 – **October:** Pianist Ronnie Ball and bassist Jimmy Gannon join Quartet, recording of Gerry Mulligan big band arrangements for Norman Granz.

1959 – JATP European tour with Wasserman, Ball, Gannon. Release of Columbia Pictures' "Gene Krupa Story" starring Sal Mineo, Krupa remarries (Patricia Bowler).

1960 – **March:** Wasserman leaves to join Gerry Mulligan. Krupa heart attack.

1961 – **March:** Wasserman rejoins for Krupa-Anita O'Day reunion gig at New York's Basin St. East. **June:** Verve recording of semi-symphonic pieces under arranger George Williams' direction.

1962 – **January:** Second studio recording of drum duel with Buddy Rich.

1963 – Original Benny Goodman Quartet reunion and RCA recording with Hampton, Wilson. **Summer:** Krupa Big Band reassembled for Disneyland dates.

1964 – **January:** Great New Quartet, featuring Ventura, pianist John Bunch and bassist Nabil Totah makes final Verve recording, later Japanese and Mexican tours.

1965 – At the beginning of the year, Quartet personnel consists of Carmen Leggio, bassist Ed DeHaas and pianist Dick Wellstood, a group that toured South America, played Vegas regularly and appeared on many local and national television shows.

1966 – Eddie Shu rejoins at year's end. Quartet makes successful Israeli tour.

1967 – After gigs at Al Hirt's in New Orleans in May, Atlantic City's Steel Pier and in Cincinnati (summer), Krupa announces retirement saying, "I feel too lousy to play and know I must sound lousy."

1969 – Began lectures at various schools against drugs, which included one talk (and drum demonstration) at the County Court Building in Mineola, New York. Began doing clinics for Slingerland Drum Company and traveled to Frankfurt, Germany Music Trade Fair on their behalf.

1970 – **June:** Came out of retirement at New York's Plaza Hotel with new Quartet (featuring Eddie Shu). Various weekend gigs with Shu (including a reunion show featuring Shu and Ventura in Philadelphia) and sit-in appearances at clubs with Dixie groups.

1972 – July: Appearances at Newport in New York Jazz Festival, including giant, all-star jam session at Radio City Music Hall. **November:** Final Krupa recording, for Hank O'Neal's Chiaroscuro Records, featuring Condon, Kenny Davern (clarinet), Wild Bill Davison (cornet), Dick Wellstood (piano), recorded live at The New School in New York. **December:** Inducted into **down beat Magazine's** "Jazz Hall of Fame."

1973 – June: Reunion of the Goodman Quartet at Carnegie Hall during Newport in New York Jazz Festival. **July 4:** Concert at Singer Bowl. **July 7:** Receives honorary plaque from Jo Jones signed by almost every living drummer. **August 18:** Last known personal appearance of Krupa — with the Goodman Quartet at the Performing Arts Center at Saratoga Springs. **October 16:** Gene Krupa dead at the age of 64 of leukemia and heart failure.

AWARDS

METRONOME MAGAZINE, "Number One Drummer": 1937, 1938, 1939, 1940, 1941, 1942, 1943, 1944, 1945.

down beat MAGAZINE, "Number One Drummer": 1936, 1937, 1938, 1943, 1952, 1953.

down beat MAGAZINE, "Hall of Fame," December, 1972.

ESQUIRE MAGAZINE, "Silver Award": 1946.

PLAYBOY MAGAZINE, "Reader's Poll": Number Two Drummer, 1960.

MODERN DRUMMER MAGAZINE, first inductee "Hall of Fame."

GENE KRUPA/COLLECTIVE PERSONNEL

**THE FIRST BAND
1938-1943**

Trumpets: Ray Cameron, Charles Frankhauser, Tom Gonsoulin, Corky Cornelius, Torg Halten, Nate Kazebier, Tom DiCarlo, Dave Schultze, Shorty Sherock, Rudy Novak, Norman Murphy, Roy Eldridge, Babe Wagner, Mickey Mangano, Al Beck, Nick Prospero, Graham Young.

Trombones: Toby Tyler, Bruce Squires, Dalton Rizzotto, Al Jordan, Red Ogle, Floyd O'Brien, Charles McCamish, Chuck Evans, Sid Brantley, Babe Wagner, Jay Kelliher, Pat Virgadame, Graham Young, Al Beck, Leo Watson, Norman Murphy, Tommy Pederson, Greg Phillips, John Grassie, Rodney Ogle, Al Sherman, Joe Conigliaro, Herbie Harper, Joe Howard.

Reeds: Bob Snyder, Musky Ruffo, Sam Musiker, Sam Donahue, Clint Neagly, Murray Williams, George Siravo, Carl Biesacker, Buddy De-Franco, Walter Bates, Vido Musso, Charlie Ventura, Jimmy Migliero, Sam Listengart, Ben Feman, Rex Kittig, Don Brassfield, Mike Simpson.

Guitar: Ray (Remo) Biondi, Teddy Walters.

Bass: Horace Rollins, Biddy Bastien, Ed Mihelich.

Piano: Milt Raskin, Bob Kitsis, Joe Springer, Dodo Marmorosa, Tony D'Amore, Bob Curtis.

Vocalists: Irene Day, Leo Watson, Anita O'Day, Howard Dulaney, Johnny Desmond, Gene Howard, Gloria Van, Lilyann Carol, Ray Eberle.

Arrangers: Chappie Willett, Fred Norman, Sam Donahue, Benny Carter, Elton Hill, Ray Biondi, Jimmy Mundy, Bert Ross, Toots Camarata, Sam Musiker.

**THE SECOND
BAND
1944-1951**

Trumpets: Don Fagerquist, Bill Conrad, Joe Triscari, Vince Hughes, Tony Russo, Pinky Savitt, Jimmy Millazzio, Red Rodney, Ray Triscari, Tony Anelli, Al Porcino, Ed Badgley, Gordon Boswell, Dick Dale, Buddy Colaneri, Ed Shedowski, Roy Eldridge, John Bello, Fern Caron, Bill Purcell, Joe Cabot, Billy Robbins, Mike Shane, Lee Katzman, Nick Travis, Leon Merian.

Trombones: Leon Cox, Tommy Pederson, Bill Culley, Dick Taylor, Andy Parker, Nick Gaglio, Bob Ascher, Tasso Harris, Warren Covington, Ben Seaman, Carl "Ziggy" Elmer, Randy Bellerjeau, Moe Schneider, Clay Hervey, Emil Mazanec, Jack Zimmerman, Urbie Green, Bob Fitzpatrick, Walter Robertson, Frank Rehak, Allan Langstaff, Frank Rosolino, Herb Randel, Gene Mullens, Rob Swope, George Roberts, Eddie Aulino, Earl Holt.

Reeds: Murray Williams, Frank Antonelli, Charlie Ventura, Andy Pino, Johnny Bothwell, Steve Bendrick, Stuart Olson, Adrian Teiz, Charlie Kennedy, Harry Terrill, Bill Hitz, Sid Brown, Buddy Wise, Joe Koch, Jack Schwartz, Joe Magro, Mitchell Melnick, Sam Marowitz, Tommy Lucas, Larry Patton, Lenny Hambro, Bob Morton, Jerry Therkeld, Carl Friend, Dale Keever, Kenny Pinson, Harvey Cousins, John Lujack, Bill Davis, Turk Tarlington, Walt Howall, Ray Davidson, Hal Feldman, Reggie Merrill, Frank Salto, Hal Lockwood, Gerry Mulligan, Robert Morton, Boots Mussilli, Gene Quill, Stan Getz.

Guitar: Ed Yance, Frank Morrell, Mike Triscari, Hy White, Stan Doughty, Bob Lesher, Ralph Blaze, Ray Biondi, Dennis Sandole.

Bass: Clyde Newcomb, Harry Babasin, Irv Lang, Bob Munoz, Bob Strahl, Peter Ruggerio, Don Simpson, George Atwood, Dante Martucci.

Piano: Teddy Napoleon, George Walters, Buddy Neal, Bill Baker, Joe Cohen, Norman Schnell, Dave Sills, Tommy Egnelli, Marty Napoleon, Harvey Leonard.

Deputy Drummers: Joe Dale, Louis Zito.

Misc. Percussion: Ramon Rivera, Hernando Bravo.

Vocalists: Ginnie Powell, Buddy Stewart, Lillian Lane, Jerry Duane, Dave Lambert, Anita O'Day, Carolyn Grey, Tom Berry, Buddy Hughes, Delores Hawkins, Peggy Mann, Bill Black, Frances Lynn, Joe Tucker, Bobby Soots, Barry Wood.

Strings: Jacob Shulman, Victor Pariante, Ray Biondi, Ted Blume, Jerome Reisler, Paul Powell, George Grossman, Julius Ehrenworth.

Arrangers: Gerry Mulligan, Eddie Finckel, Budd Johnson, Neal Hefti, George Williams, Sy Oliver, Grey Rains, Don Simpson.

SMALL GROUPS 1952-1973 (excluding all-star combinations for recordings and concerts)

Reeds: Eddie Shu (tenor and alto saxophones, clarinet, trumpet, harmonica), Charlie Ventura (alto, tenor, baritone and bass saxophones), Carmen Leggio (tenor saxophone), Eddie Wasserman (clarinet, tenor saxophone and flute), Flip Phillips (tenor saxophone), Gale Curtis (clarinet).

Piano: Teddy Napoleon, Ronnie Ball, Bobby Scott, Dick Wellstood, John Bunch, Dave McKenna, Dave Frishberg, Dill Jones, John Gambra, Marty Napoleon, Jay Chaison.

Bass: John Drew, Whitey Mitchell, Bill Takas, Benny Moten, Dave Pearlman, Nabil "Knobby" Totah, Jimmy Gannon, Mort Herbert, Eddie DeHaas, Scotty Holt.

GENE KRUPA/FILMOGRAPHY *denotes home video availability

WITH BENNY GOODMAN AND HIS ORCHESTRA	**The Big Broadcast of 1937**/Produced in 1936/100 minutes/director: Mitchell Leisen. **Hollywood Hotel**/Produced in 1937/110 minutes/director: Busby Berkely. **Hooray for Hollywood**/Produced in 1976/110 minutes/director: unknown/ Compilation film ala "That's Entertainment" with Goodman-Krupa clip from "Hollywood Hotel."
GENE KRUPA AND HIS OR-CHESTRA	**Gene Krupa, America's Ace Drummer Man and his Orchestra**/Produced in 1941/10 minutes/director: Leslie Roush/Vocalists Howard Dulaney and Irene Day in three tunes, including *Jungle Madness.* **Sugar Hill Masquerade**/Produced in 1942/director: unknown/Soundie, other details unknown. **Book Revue**/Produced in 1945/seven minutes/director: Robert Clampett/ Warner Brothers' "Blue Ribbon" cartoon, featuring caricatures of Goodman, Dorsey, James and Krupa. **Eddie Condon's Floor Show**/Produced in 1949/20 minutes/director: unknown/featurette produced for television, with a group including Roy Eldridge and Peanuts Hucko. **Steve Allen in Movieland**/Produced in 1955/running time and director unknown/Originally produced for NBC television as three-tune promo for "The Benny Goodman Story." **Jamming with Gene Krupa**/Produced in 1959/running time and director unknown/Globe Video Pictures produced this promo short for *The Gene Krupa Story* which focuses on Krupa's "teaching" Sal Mineo in finer points of drumming. ***Thanks for the Boogie Ride**/Produced in 1942/three minutes/director: unknown/Soundie short featuring Anita O'Day and Roy Eldridge. **Gene Krupa**/three minutes/Soundie short #9505/details unknown. ***Let Me Off Uptown**/Produced in 1942/three minutes/director: unknown/ Soundie short featuring Anita O'Day and Roy Eldridge. ***Follow That Music**/Produced in 1946/18 minutes/director: Arthur Dreifuss/The Krupa Band and Jazz Trio featuring pianist Marty Napoleon, Red Rodney, Gerry Mulligan. ***Drummer Man**/Produced in 1947/15 minutes/director: Will Cowan/ Featuring vocalist Carolyn Grey, dancer Jeanne Blanche, the Trio and full band. Tunes include *Lover, Boogie Blues, Stompin' at the Savoy, Blanchette,* and *Leave Us Leap.*

*Featuring Gene Krupa and His Orchestra/Produced in 1948/10 minutes/ director: unknown/"Thrills of Music" series with tunes including *Bop Boogie, Sabre Dance,* and *Disc Jockey Jump.*

*Deep Purple/Produced in 1949/15 minutes/director: Will Cowan/ Saxophonists Lenny Hambro and Buddy Wise featured in *Lemon Drop, Deep Purple, Bop Boogie, Melody in F.*

*Gene Krupa and His Orchestra/Produced in 1949/15 minutes/director: Will Cowan/Trombonist-vocalist Frank Rosolino (billed as Frankie Ross) featured on *Lemon Drop*, other tunes include *Bop Boogie*, and *Deep Purple*.

Many of these clips are now available on home video via Anita O'Day's Las Vegas-based Emily Productions, and on MCA'S *Best of the Big Bands* compilation.

DOCUMEN-TARIES	**March of Time**, 10th Year/Produced in 1944/16 minutes/director: unknown/ "Music in America" series. Benny Goodman, featuring Krupa, plays *Henderson Stomp*. **Feather on Jazz**/Produced in 1967/half-hour episodes/Produced by Leonard Feather/MCA Television compilation of clips from Paramount, Universal, still photos and recordings, Krupa featured in clip from "Rhythm Romance." **American Music - From Folk to Jazz and Pop**/Produced in 1969/49 minutes/director: Stephen Fleishman/Pop music history with section on jazz featuring Krupa, Ellington, Goodman, etc. *Born to Swing/Produced in 1973, England/50 minutes/director: John Jeremy/Krupa, many ex-Basieites extensively featured.
FEATURE FILMS	**Some Like it Hot**/Produced in 1938/65 minutes/director: George Archainbaud/Krupa second-billed to Bob Hope, many tunes by first edition of First Band, plus Krupa in speaking role. Retitled "Rhythm Romance." *Ball of Fire/Produced in 1941/112 minutes/director: Howard Hawks/Comedy with Barbara Stanwyck and Gary Cooper, with Krupa band featured in *Drum Boogie*. After vocal by Stanwyck, Krupa switches from drumsticks to matchsticks for his solo. The finale? The matches burst into flames. **Syncopation**/Produced in 1942/88 minutes/director: William Dieterle/ Appearances by Krupa band, Benny Goodman, Charlie Barnet, Joe Venuti, Harry James, Rex Stewart, etc. *George White's Scandals/Produced in 1945/95 minutes/director: Felix E. Feist/The Second Band with strings in a few numbers, including *Bolero in the Jungle, Leave Us Leap*.

Beat the Band/Produced in 1947/67 minutes/director: John H. Auer/The Second Band, with Gerry Mulligan on alto sax, featured on *Shadow Rhapsody*, among others, plus Krupa in a supporting role.

*Boy! What a Girl/Produced in 1947/70 minutes/director: unknown/All-black musical cast — Slam Stewart, Sidney Catlett, etc., with special guest appearance by Krupa.

Smart Politics/Produced in 1948/68 minutes/director: Will Jason/ Monogram programmer featuring Freddie Stewart, June Preisser and The Harmonica Boys.

Glamor Girl/Produced in 1948/68 minutes/director: Arthur Dreifuss/The Second Band featured in *Gene's Boogie, Anywhere.*

Make Believe Ballroom/Produced in 1949/78 minutes/director: Joseph Santley/Last film appearance of Krupa with his own big band. Other groups include Jimmy Dorsey, Pee Wee Hunt, Charlie Barnet and Nat Cole.

*The Glenn Miller Story/Produced in 1953/116 minutes/director: Anthony Mann/Krupa featured with Louis Armstrong group in *Dark Eyes,* and drum duel with Cozy Cole on *Basin Street Blues*.

*The Benny Goodman Story/Produced in 1955/116 minutes/director: Valentine Davies/Krupa featured throughout playing himself in speaking role, and as sideman and featured soloist in Goodman Band.

*The Gene Krupa Story/Produced in 1959/99 minutes/director: Don Weis/Sal Mineo in the title role with drums recorded by Krupa. Krupa himself can be glimpsed in early "parlor" scene behind a doorway when Mineo brings in his first drum set.

*Jazz Ball/Produced in 1956/60 minutes/director: Herbert L. Bregstein/Compilation of Soundie material, various clips featuring Krupa bands.

*One Night Stand with Lionel Hampton/Produced for Canadian television in 1971, now on home video from Independent United Distributors (and other labels). The 50-minute, color, stereo production features Mel Torme', Hampton, Buddy Rich, Teddy Wilson and many others.

PRIMARY SOURCE: *Jazz in the Movies, A Guide to Jazz Musicians 1917- 1977*, by David Meeker, Talisman Books (London), 1972.

GENE KRUPA/SELECTED ALBUM TITLES

This listing is by no means all-inclusive. With spotty availability of various bootlegs of the big bands and small groups, and seemingly more coming out each month, compiling such a list would be nearly impossible. The most complete discographies are George Hall's work for Jazz Discographies, Unlimited; Charles Garrod's and Bill Korst's for Joyce Music, and Ernst Ronowski's Krupa Discography, published in West Germany. Detailed here are long-playing albums by Gene Krupa as a big band and small group leader, as well as titles where he played a featured role as a part of an all-star combination. Note: Many small group recordings on Verve were first issued on 10 or 12-inch Clef/Norgran recordings. Norman Granz later consolidated many sessions on reissues under the Verve banner. Hence, only the later Verve items are detailed here, except when **only** issued on Clef or Norgran.

Drummin' Man (Columbia C2L-29)

BIG BAND ANTHOLOGIES

The finest of the anthologies, covering the years 1938-1949.

Gene Krupa and his Orchestra On the Air (Aircheck 35)
1944-1946 tracks, including first radio broadcast of the Second Band and 1943 V-Discs of the first Trio with Buddy DeFranco and Dodo Marmorosa.

That Drummer's Band (Epic/Encore Series EE22027)
Superb sides from the First Band, 1940-1942.

That Drummer's Band (Sounds of Swing LP-114)
Various tracks, 1939-1941, 1944, 1946, 1947.

That Drummer's Band (VSP-4)
Budget Verve compilation of 1956 O'Day-Eldridge reunion, and 1959 *Krupa Plays Mulligan* sides.

Gene Krupa/His Orchestra and The Jazz Trio (Swing House SWH-40)
The years 1941, 1944, 1945, 1946.

The Greatest Big Band Combining Swing and Be-Bop (Renkcurb 11D1810)
The years 1944-1951.

Challenging the Challenger (First Heard FH 35)
1945 tracks with strings.

Gene Krupa and his Orchestra/1942-1943 Broadcasts (Fanfare 44-144)
Tracks highlighted by singer Ray Eberle's brief stint with the band.

One Night Stand with Gene Krupa/1945-1946 (Joyce 1137)

Gene Krupa Featuring Roy Eldridge and Anita O'Day (Fanfare 10-110) 1938-1942 air checks.

Gene Krupa and his Orchestra from Meadowbrook Gardens (Fanfare 34-134)
Two 1946 air checks.
Wire Brush Stomp (Bandstand 7117)
The First Bands of 1938-1941.
One Night Stand with Gene Krupa/1940 and 1946 (Joyce 1107)
To Be or Not to Be-Bop (Sounds of Swing LP-119)
Covering the years 1938-1949.
King Krupa (Swing Treasury 106)
1945 air shots heavily featuring Charlie Ventura, Anita O'Day, Buddy Stewart.
Gene Krupa and His Orchestra 1946-1947 (First Time Records 1512)
Gene Krupa at The Click (JRC-1208)
1944 and 1947 airchecks.
IAJRC-10
Issued through the International Association of Jazz Record Collectors, covering the years 1945-1946.
The Exciting Gene Krupa (Giants of Jazz 1028)
10/2/44 and 8/15/45 sessions.
Gene Krupa's Sidekicks (Columbia Special Projects JCL641)
Covering the years 1938-1949.
Ace Drummer Man (Giants of Jazz 1006)
1944 and 1945 Trio tracks, 1945 and 1947 big bands.
What's This (Hep 20)
Covering the years 1946-1947.
Gene Krupa and His Orchestra 1949 (Alamac QSR-2450)
Live Hollywood recordings 4/5, 8/12/49.
Gene Krupa in Disco Order Volume 21 (Ajaz-241)
Ajaz has chronicled practically the entire recorded career of Krupa in some 23 volumes. This one features the final big band sides originally issued on RCA, recorded 1/26, 5/9/49, and 2/24, 3/20/50.
Swingin' With Krupa (RCA Camden 340)
Three separate sessions: Krupa's first-ever recordings as a leader in November, 1935, produced by John Hammond for English Parlaphone; the "Dixie/commercial sides" featuring vocalist Bobby Soots done for RCA in March and September, 1950; and the "Krupa Plays Fats Waller" big band sides (also included on the Ajaz volume) of 2/24/50.
Gene Krupa and His Orchestra with Anita O'Day and Roy Eldridge (Verve 2008)

Reunion produced by Norman Granz 2/56, with "modernized" charts arranged by Manny Albam, Nat Pierce, Billy Byers and Quincy Jones. Subsequently issued on English Verve Select 2317113. On April 27, four more big band sides were recorded in Los Angeles under arranger Buddy Bregman, which included the Krupa Quartet of that time and the vocal group The Wailers. Issued on Verve 2016.

Gene Krupa Plays Gerry Mulligan Arrangements (Verve 8292)

Produced by Norman Granz 10/20 and 11/20/58, subsequently issued on English Verve Select 2317113. Three non-Mulligan big band tracks, arranged and conducted by George Williams, were recorded for Verve on 11/1/58, but were never issued.

The Gene Krupa Story (Verve Celebrity 15010)

1959 recordings from the motion picture sound track arranged and conducted by Leith Stevens.

Film Tracks of Buddy Rich and Gene Krupa (Joyce 3002)

1938 "Some Like it Hot" tracks and two tracks taken directly from audio portion of "Gene Krupa Story."

Classic in Percussion (Verve 8450)

6/5, 6/12, 6/16/61 semi-classical pieces with four-man percussion section arranged by George Williams. Also issued under the title *Percussion King* on Verve 8414.

Hot Drums (Stack-O-Hits AG9048)

Budget repackaging, beefed up with echo and phony stereo, of Alamac QSR2450.

Verve's Choice The Best of Gene Krupa (Verve 8594)

Small group tracks 1950-1959, one track each from "Krupa Plays Mulligan" and "Classics in Percussion."

The World's Greatest Drummer 1952-1961 (Sunbeam SB-225)

The Japanese Trio sessions of 1952, The Quartet featuring Eddie Shu at the Steel Pier in 1956, The Quartet featuring Eddie Wasserman from "Playboy's Penthouse" television show 4/7/61, jam session featuring Buck Clayton, Pee Wee Russell and Eddie Wasserman from "Philadelphia Jazz Festival" at Connie Mack Stadium 8/28/60.

Gene Krupa (MGM Golden Archive Series GAS-132)

Small groups and all-star combinations of 1950-1958.

Gene Krupa (Metro 518)

Compilation of mid-fifties small groups, 1956 Verve recreations and "Classics in Percussion" tracks.

Rare Live Performances/The Gene Krupa Quartet (Swing House SWH-21)

Chicago London House sessions featuring Eddie Wasserman 3/3, 3/10/61; and Charlie Ventura's first appearances with The Great New Quartet at the Steel Pier 8/30/62.

SMALL GROUP ANTHOLOGIES

THE WORKING GROUPS

The Gene Krupa Trio Collates (Clef MGC-121/10-inch)

Recorded 3/19/52, and featuring Charlie Ventura (tenor and bass sax), Teddy Napoleon (piano).

Gene Krupa in Disco Order Volume 23 (Ajaz 262)

Incorporated 3/19/52 sessions and 4/18/52 Japanese sessions. Personnel as Clef 121.

Gene Krupa/Marty Napoleon/Charlie Ventura (Ozone 25)

Bootleg Trio sessions recorded between March and April, 1952, possibly at Officer's Club in Hawaii. Teddy Napoleon is the pianist, not Marty as indicated on the cover.

Norman Granz Jazz at the Philharmonic featuring the Gene Krupa Trio

(Verve 8031)

Recorded 6/52, and featuring Charlie Ventura (tenor sax only), Teddy Napoleon (piano).

Sing, Sing, Sing (Verve 8190)

Recorded 12/26/53, and featuring Eddie Shu (tenor and also sax, trumpet, clarinet and harmonica), Teddy Napoleon (piano).

Gene Krupa Quartet (Clef MGC-668)

Recorded 12/15/54 and 2/15/55, and featuring Eddie Shu (tenor and alto sax, clarinet and trumpet), Bobby Scott (piano), John Drew (bass).

The Jazz Rhythms of Gene Krupa (Verve 8204)

Recorded 12/15/54, and featuring Eddie Shu (tenor and alto sax, clarinet and trumpet), Dave McKenna (piano), Wendell Marshall (bass).

Hey, Here's Gene Krupa (Verve 8300)

Recorded 5/57, and featuring Eddie Shu (tenor and alto sax, clarinet and trumpet), Dave McKenna (piano), Wendell Marshall (bass).

Krupa Rocks (Verve 8276)

Recorded 9/57, and featuring Gale Curtis (clarinet), Teddy Napoleon (piano), Mort Herbert (bass).

Big Noise from Winnetka (Verve 8310)

Recorded live at Chicago's London House 1/59, and featuring Eddie Wasserman (tenor sax, clarinet and flute), Ronnie Ball (piano), Jimmy Gannon (bass).

Carmen Leggio

Krupa saxophonist Leggio (1964-1966) produced and marketed this album, which features the "never-commercially-recorded" Krupa group of the time on three tracks. The Quartet is rounded out by bassist Benny Moten and pianist John Gambra. Last available via Carmen Leggio, Box #64, Tarrytown, New York 10591.

Broadcast Tributes (BTRIB-0006)
New Year's Eve, 1966, from The Metropole, with Leggio, Eddie De-Hass (bass), Dick Wellstood (piano) playing *Dark Eyes* and *Flyin' Home*.
The Great New Gene Krupa Quartet featuring Charlie Ventura (Verve 8584)
Recorded 1/20, 2/5/64, and featuring Charlie Ventura (alto, tenor, baritone and bass sax), John Bunch (piano), Nabil "Knobby" Totah (bass).
Gene Krupa and His Men of Jazz (Star Line Productions SLC-61006)
Not listed in any discography and available only on cassette, a 1958 set from St. Louis' Sheraton-Jefferson Hotel. Featuring Eddie Wasserman (reeds), Ronnie Ball (piano), probably Jimmy Gannon (bass).
The Swingin' Gene Krupa Quartet (Star Line Productions SG-8019)
More never-issued London House sessions from 1959, plus a duplication of the two 1966 Broadcast Tributes sides.
Gene Krupa/Ace Drummer Man Volume Two (Star Line Productions SLC-6107)
Another tape only set, "Dial M for Music" television broadcast of 1967 with Eddie Shu (tenor, alto sax and harmonica), Hal McKinney (piano), Benny Moten (bass).

AT JAZZ AT THE PHILHARMONIC

Norman Granz Presents Original - Volume I - Jazz At The Philharmonic
(Stinson SLP-23)
The first recorded JATP concert, 2/12/45, and featuring Charlie Ventura and Illinois Jacquet (tenor sax), Joe Guy and Howard McGhee (trumpet), Willie Smith (alto sax), Ulysses Livingston (guitar), Garland Finney (piano), Red Callendar (bass). Krupa billed for contractual reasons as "Chicago Flash" on original 78 issues, no drummer credited on Stinson LP notes.
The Drum Battle/Gene Krupa and Buddy Rich at Jazz At The Philharmonic
(Verve 8369)
Recorded 10/11/52, and featuring Willie Smith (alto sax), Hank Jones (piano). The battle with Rich was the first recorded duel between the two, the only one to be captured live. Subsequently issued - not in its original form - on Verve (polydor) 815-146-1.
Jazz At The Philharmonic Volume 9 (Verve)
Recorded 9/23/53, and featuring Benny Carter (alto sax), Oscar Peterson (piano).
Jazz At The Philharmonic in Tokyo/Live at the Nichigeki Theater)
(Pablo Live 2620 104)

Recorded 11/18/53, same personnel as above.

Jazz At The Philharmonic/The Rarest Concerts (Verve/Polydor 845 149 1)

Recorded in 1953 (month and day unknown), and one of the rare times Krupa appeared in the jam session context at JATP, rather than Trio leader. Featuring Charlie Shavers and Roy Eldridge (trumpet), Willie Smith and Benny Carter (alto sax), Flip Phillips and Ben Webster (tenor sax), Bill Harris (trombone), Oscar Peterson (organ and piano), Herb Ellis (guitar), Ray Brown (bass).

The Gene Krupa Quartet/Max Roach-Clifford Brown Quintet (Hall of Fame Jazz Greats 633)

Recorded 10/2/55, and featuring Eddie Shu (tenor sax, clarinet and trumpet), Bobby Scott (piano), John Drew (bass). Some of these tracks are reportedly a part of Jazz At The Philharmonic Volume 11.

NOTE: Among the rarest of Krupa recordings were recorded as a part of the JATP troupe in Vasteras, Sweden, on 7/25/52, and featured Flip Phillips in the Trio's reed chair and Teddy Napoleon on piano. According to Jorgen Grunnet Jepsen's 9/70 discography, these were issued overseas on the Selecta label. Some discographers indicate only short "test pressings" are known to exist.

ALL STAR COMBINATIONS

The Benny Goodman Show, with Martha Tilton and Gene Krupa (Sunbeam SM- 151)

7/29/46 broadcast featuring guest star Krupa with Goodman Trio, giving comedic "drum lesson" to host Peter Donald, and in short drum duel with then-current Goodman drummer Louis Bellson.

Benny Goodman Trio Plays for Fletcher Henderson Fund (Columbia 516)

1950 session, the first recorded reunion of the original BG Trio, with guest stars including bassist Eddie Safranski, guitarist Johnny Smith, trombonist Lou McGarity, trumpeter Buck Clayton.

The Exciting Gene Krupa (Verve 8071)

Recorded 5/7, 9/27,53, and featuring Charlie Shavers (trumpet), Bill Harris (trombone), Ben Webster (tenor sax), Teddy Wilson (piano), Herb Ellis (guitar), Ray Brown (bass). These tracks, as well as four sides recorded 5/7 which featured Shavers, Wilson, plus Steve Jordon (guitar) and Israel Crosby (bass), were originally issued on Clef 10-inch LPs, entitled "The Gene Krupa Sextets," Volumes 1-3.

The Driving Gene Krupa (Verve 8107)

Recorded 11/12/53, and featuring Charlie Shavers (trumpet), Bill Harris (trombone), Eddie "Lockjaw" Davis (tenor sax), Teddy Napoleon (piano), Ray Brown (bass).

Jam Session at Carnegie Hall (Columbia CL 557)
1957 benefit concert with all-star bandsmen including Buck Clayton, Ruby Braff (trumpets); Urbie Green and Vernon Brown (trombones); Tony Scott (clarinet), Lem Davis, Buddy Tate and Eddie Shu (reeds); Mel Powell and Teddy Napoleon (piano); Steve Jordon (guitar); Milt Hinton (bass); Jo Jones (drums).

Krupa/Hampton/Wilson Quartet (Verve 8066)
Recorded 7/31/55 during the filming of *The Benny Goodman Story*. Bassist Red Callendar made the trio a quartet.

Krupa and Rich (Verve 8069)
Recorded 11/1/55 - the first in-studio, Krupa-Rich drum duel and featuring Roy Eldridge and Dizzy Gillespie (trumpet), Flip Phillips and Illinois Jacquet (tenor sax), Oscar Peterson (piano), Herb Ellis (guitar), Ray Brown (bass).

Timex All Star Jazz Show #1 (Sounds Great 8005)
1957 television special, with Charlie Ventura/Bobby Scott/Krupa reunion Trio playing *Dark Eyes*.

The Second Timex All Star Jazz Show (Radiola/Music Series release-1095)
1958 television special, with Krupa and Lionel Hampton backing singer Jaye P. Morgan.

The Swingin' Years (Sandy Hook 2087)
1960 television show, hosted by Ronald Reagan, with Krupa, O'Day and studio band playing *Drum Boogie*.

Jack Teagarden/His Sextet and Condon's Chicagoans (Pumpkin 115)
1961 television shots reuniting the Chicago Gang, with Jimmy McPartland (cornet), Teagarden (trombone), Pee Wee Russell (clarinet), Bud Freeman (tenor saxophone), Eddie Condon (guitar), Bob Haggart (bass).

Burnin' Beat/Gene Krupa-Buddy Rich (Verve 8471)
Recorded 1/18, 1/19/62 and featuring Joe Wilder, Nick Travis, Don Goldie and Al Stewart (trumpet); Frank Rehak and Jimmy Cleveland (trombone); Sam Marowitz, Eddie Wasserman, Gerry Sanfino and Danny Bank (reeds), George Barnes and Howard Collins (guitar); John Bunch (piano); Trigger Alpert (bass).

Drum Beat for Dancing Feet/Cozy Cole and His Orchestra (Coral 75723)
Recorded circa 1962 and featuring four drummers - Krupa, Cole, Panama Francis and Ray McKinley - in dance arrangements under the direction of Henry Jerome.

Tony Bennett and Gene Krupa (Sunbeam P-509)
Recorded 1963 as a promotional program for the National Guard hosted by Martin Block. Featuring Eddie Wasserman (tenor sax,

clarinet, flute), John Bunch (piano), probably Bill Takas (bass). Additional tracks from these sessions are available on "Tony Bennett Meets Gene Krupa" (Sandy Hook S-2067).

The Mighty Two/Louis Bellson and Gene Krupa (Roulette Birdland R-52098)

Recorded in 1963 as a drum instruction record for rudimental studies as applied to jazz (printed drum parts were available at the time by mail). Personnel includes Joe Newman (trumpet), Seldon Powell (tenor sax), Dick Hyman (piano), Mary Osbourne (guitar), Milt Hinton and Art Davis (bass). Bellson writer-arranger Fred Thompson arranged and scored.

Together Again! The Benny Goodman Quartet (RCA 2698)

Recorded in 1964 - the first recorded reunion of the original BG quartet, featuring Benny Goodman (clarinet), Lionel Hampton (vibraphone), Teddy Wilson (piano).

Jazz at the New School (Chiaroscuro CR-110)

Recorded in November, 1972, Gene Krupa's last commercially issued recording. Featuring Kenny Davern (clarinet and soprano sax), Wild Bill Davidson (trumpet), Eddie Condon (guitar), Dick Wellstood (piano).

INDEX

ORDER FORM

Pathfinder Publishing
of California
458 Dorothy Ave.
Ventura, CA 93003
Telephone (805)642-9278   FAX 805-650-3656

Please send me the following books from Pathfinder Publishing:

_____Copies of *Agony & Death on a
   Gold Rush Steamer* @ $8.95 $_____
_____Copies of *Beyond Sympathy* @ $9.95 $_____
_____Copies of *Dialogues In Swing* @ $12.95 $_____
_____Copies of *Living Creatively
   With Chronic Illness* @ $11.95 $_____
_____Copies of *No Time For Goodbyes* @ $8.95 $_____
_____Copies of *Marlin Justice* Soft Cover @ $9.95 $_____
_____Copies of *Marlin Justice* Hard Cover @ $16.95 $_____
_____Copies of *Quest For Respect* @ $6.95 $_____
_____Copies of *Stop Justice Abuse* @ $10.95 $_____
_____Copies of *Shipwrecks, Smugglers and Maritime
   Mysteries* @ $9.95 $_____
_____Copies of *World of Gene Krupa* @ $14.95 $_____
_____Copies of *Shipwreck Chart* @ *$3.95*   *$*_____
_____Copies of *Hist. Map of Santa Barbara Co.* @ $3.95 $_____
_____Copies of *Historical Map of Ventura Co.* @ $3.95 $_____
                              Sub-Total $_____
        Discount $_____
        Californians: Please add 6.25% tax. $_____
        Shipping & Handling* $_____
                              Grand Total $_____

I understand that I may return the book for a full refund if
not satisfied.
Name:_____
Organization:_____
Address:_____
_____ZIP:_____

*SHIPPING CHARGES U.S.
Books: Enclose $2.25 for the first book and .50c for each
additional book. UPS: Truck; $3.25 for first item, .50c for each
additional. UPS Air: $4.50 for first item, $1.25 for each
additional item. Alaska and Hawaii: $6.75 for first book, $1.50
for each additional. Maps: $2.00 for the first 6 maps, and .50c
for each additional 6 maps.